Haydn Richards
Junior English · 2
Revised edition

Revised by Angela Burt
Adviser: Patricia Lewis

GINN

Acknowledgements

Grateful acknowlegement is made to the following for permission to use copyright material:

page 12 **Raman meets the rocking-horse**
The Rocking-Horse by Rosemary Manning.
By kind permission of Hamish Hamilton Ltd.

18 **Some useful finds**
The Bicycle Wheel by Ruth Ainsworth.
By kind permission of Hamish Hamilton Ltd.

24 **Magic balloons**
My First Science Book by Angela Wilkes, published by Dorling Kindersley.
By kind permission of Dorling Kindersley Holdings plc.

30 **Lone Dog**
"Lone Dog" by Irene Rutherford McLeod, from *Songs to Save a Soul* by Irene Rutherford McLeod, published by Chatto and Windus.
By kind permission of the Estate of Irene Rutherford McLeod.

78 **Feeding the Cats**
"Feeding the Cats" © Fleur Adcock.
By kind permission of Fleur Adcock.

84 **A bear cub's adventure**
Baby Mishook by Leon Golschmann.
By kind permission of Bodley Head.

Every effort has been made to complete the above list of acknowledgements. The publishers would be grateful for any discrepancies to be notified.

Designed by Michael Soderberg with Alan Miller
Illustrated by Barry Rowe, Martin White, Beverly Curl, Vali Herzer and Hardlines

© Haydn Richards 1965
Revised edition 1997
Fourth impression 1998

ISBN 0 602 27510 5   (without answers)
ISBN 0 602 27511 3   (with answers)

Published by Ginn and Company
Prebendal House, Parson's Fee
Aylesbury, Bucks HP20 2QY
Ginn on the Internet http://www.ginn.co.uk

Filmset by Wyvern Typesetting Ltd, Bristol
Printed in Great Britain at the University Press, Cambridge

Preface to the Revised Edition

This revised and updated edition of Haydn Richards' popular series meets the appropriate requirements of the 1995 National Curriculum for English at Key Stage 1 and Key Stage 2. It is also in line with the requirements of the Northern Ireland and Scottish 5-14 curricula.

Particular care has been taken while incorporating changes to preserve the successful format, tone and clarity of the original series.

Those already familiar with Junior English will see that in this revised edition there is now increased coverage of spelling, punctuation and grammar topics in each of the four books and that formal grammatical terminology, in response to popular request, is now used from the very beginning. Throughout the series, both the range and complexity of the reading comprehension exercises have been extended. Additional vocabulary exercises have been introduced together with a number of dictionary practice exercises to encourage the early use of dictionaries and thesauruses.

The series, as well as preparing pupils for National Curriculum assessment, also provides a sound basis for those preparing for 11+ English entrance examinations to independent schools. The current ISEB 11+ English syllabus was taken into account during the revision of Junior English.

Angela Burt

Contents

Nouns naming words

The dog followed the boy.
Dog is the **name** of an animal.
Boy is the **name** of a person.

**A noun is the name of a
person or thing.**

A Find the nouns in these sentences.
Write them in your book.

1 The window was broken.

2 I lost my knife.

3 This pencil is too short.

4 The cake was stale.

5 The bird flew away.

6 The sea beat against the rocks.

7 The dog barked at the postman.

8 Summer is the warmest season.

9 The plane landed safely.

10 Only one apple was left in the dish.

B Name three things you might find in –

1 a toy shop   5 a car

2 a farmyard   6 a hospital

3 a kitchen   7 a cinema

4 a railway station   8 a church

Use your dictionary.

Verbs doing words

The butcher cut the meat and weighed it.

The words **cut** and **weighed** tell us what the butcher **did** to the meat.

These are **doing** words, or **action** words.

A verb is a word which shows action.

A   Find the verbs in these sentences. Write them in your book.

1   The little girl cried.

2   We cut a lot of wood for the fire.

3   Please pass me the jam.

4   Roy knocked at the door of the office.

5   Two robins hopped on to the window-ledge.

6   Preshani put her toys away and went to bed.

7   After school John cycles to the park and plays cricket.

8   The clown smiled when we waved to him.

9   Harry broke his arm when he fell off his bicycle.

10   Kirsty ate four sweets and gave the rest away.

B   Name three actions which might be done by each of these persons.

Example   a baby   cry, play, suck

1   a doctor

2   a footballer

3   your teacher

4   a gardener

5   a cricketer

6   a policeman

7   a pupil in your class

8   a farmer

Vowels

Instead of **a** always write **an** before words beginning with

a e i o u

These letters are called **vowels**.

acorn
anchor
apple
apron
arch
arm
arrow
axe
easel
eel
egg
envelope
eye
island
oar
orange
orchard

A Write the names of these things, putting **an** before each.
You will find them in the list on the left.

B Write **a** or **an** before each of these words.

1	___ book	9	___ chair
2	___ ant	10	___ organ
3	___ apple	11	___ ox
4	___ rock	12	___ elf
5	___ oval	13	___ sweet
6	___ egg	14	___ hat
7	___ flag	15	___ imp
8	___ inn	16	___ shoe

C Write **a** or **an** to finish the sentences.

1 Pauline ate ___ apple and ___ banana.

2 I will give you ___ invitation tomorrow.

3 We came to ___ lake with ___ island in the middle.

4 Lucy is spending ___ holiday with ___ aunt in London.

5 ___ east wind is colder than ___ west wind.

Verbs adding -ed and -ing

A   Write **-ing** after each word.

1	look	4	teach	7	read
2	walk	5	pay	8	camp
3	push	6	go	9	wear

B   Write **-ed** after each word.

1	stay	4	rush	7	fill
2	post	5	touch	8	end
3	work	6	help	9	turn

C   Write **-ing** after each word.
Drop the **e** at the end.
Example   serve   serving

1	blaze	4	love	7	raise
2	dance	5	share	8	hope
3	dare	6	waste		

D   Write **-ed** after each word.
Drop the **e** at the end.
Example   place   placed

1	taste	4	hate	7	snore
2	live	5	chase	8	close
3	rattle	6	blame		

E   Write the missing words by adding **-ing** or **-ed** to the verbs in bold type.

1   We saw a small dog ____ a cat.   **chase**

2   The fire ____ when a log was put on it.   **blaze**

3   The old man was ____ most of the night.   **snore**

4   Nobody ____ to answer the door.   **dare**

5   Paul sat on the rug ____ the cat.   **stroke**

6   We got there just as the shop was ____ .   **close**

camping

Adjectives describing words

The team wore red shirts.

The word **red** tells us **what kind** of **shirts** the team wore.

Because it describes the noun **shirts**, we call it an **adjective**.

An adjective is a word which describes a noun.

A   Pick out and write the adjectives in these sentences.

1   A big lorry was parked outside the school.

2   The sky became very dark before the storm broke.

3   Claire wore a new dress at the party.

4   The baby was playing with a huge teddy bear.

5   The torch gave a brilliant light.

6   The captain of the ship had a wooden leg.

7   They made an easy crossing of the shallow river.

8   We helped the blind man across the road.

9   It was such a busy street.

10   You always think you're so clever.

B   Choose an adjective from the list on the left to fill each of the spaces below.

loud	sharp
tidy	white
heavy	savage
juicy	leather
deep	beautiful

1   a ___ doll   6   a ___ pear

2   a ___ knife   7   a ___ belt

3   a ___ noise   8   a ___ room

4   a ___ dog   9   a ___ sheet

5   a ___ load   10   a ___ cut

Cinderella

Cinderella ran to the garden and brought her godmother the finest pumpkin she could find, wondering how this would help her to go to the ball.

The godmother scooped out the inside of the pumpkin, leaving nothing but the rind. Then she touched it with her magic wand, and the pumpkin was changed in a moment into a fine coach, all shining with gold.

After that she went to look into the mouse-trap, where she found six mice, all alive. She told Cinderella to lift the trap-door up a little, and as each mouse came out she gave it a tap with her wand. At once it was changed into a beautiful horse. This made a very fine team of six horses, all dappled grey in colour.

Tales from Perrault

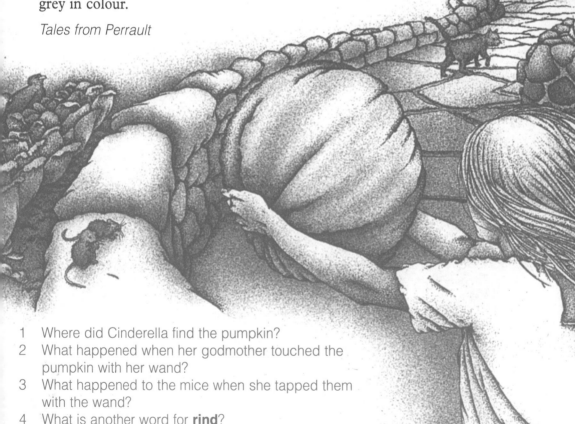

1 Where did Cinderella find the pumpkin?
2 What happened when her godmother touched the pumpkin with her wand?
3 What happened to the mice when she tapped them with the wand?
4 What is another word for **rind**?
5 Does **dappled** mean
   a smooth and silky?
   b having spots and patches of a different colour?
   c striped like a tabby cat?

6

Questions

Every question must have a **question mark (?)** at the end.

Examples
Why were you so late?
Where have you been?

why
have
who
when
how
did
what
which
whose
where

Use the words in the list on the left to fill the spaces in the questions below.

Remember to put a question mark (?) at the end of each question.

A

1 ____ you enjoy the tea

2 ____ are you today

3 ____ told you about the party

4 ____ were you absent yesterday

5 ____ did you have for dinner

6 ____ are you coming to see me

7 ____ of these books do you like best

8 ____ has Mum put the sweets

9 ____ cap is this

10 ____ you been to London

B Write five sentences of your own, each beginning with one of the words from the list above.

C Copy these sentences. Put a full stop at the end of each statement and a question mark at the end of each question.

1 I have lost my anorak

2 Did you find your cat

3 Are you feeling all right

4 Paula is a vegetarian

5 Does anyone know today's date

6 Can you help me

7 Donna collects matchboxes

7

The weather

When the weather is wet,
We must not fret.
When the weather is cold,
We must not scold.
When the weather is warm
We must not storm,
But be thankful together
Whatever the weather.

A   The words in the list on the left are used to describe weather. Write these sentences in your book, filling each space with a word from the list.

breezy
stormy
foggy
sunny
rainy
windy
misty
icy
showery
thundery

1   When the wind is blowing hard it is ___ .

2   When the sun is shining it is ___ .

3   When there is a fog it is ___ .

4   When there is a mist it is ___ .

5   When the rain pours it is a ___ day.

6   When there is a storm it is ___ .

7   When there is a breeze it is ___ .

8   When there is thunder it is ___ .

9   When there are showers the weather is ___ .

10   When the wind is as cold as ice it is ___ .

B   Write two or three sentences about any two of these.

1   a sunny morning   4   a windy day

2   a cold afternoon   5   a stormy sea

3   a wet afternoon   6   a foggy night

showeryfoggy*icy*sunny*windy*

Using the right word

has
James **has** two pet rats.
one

have
Cats **have** whiskers.
more than one

did
He **did** his work well.

done
He has **done** his work well.
helping word **has**

is
This apple **is** sour.
one

are
These apples **are** sour.
more than one

was
The boy **was** happy.
one

were
The boys **were** happy.
more than one

saw
We **saw** the Tower of London.

seen
We have **seen** the Tower of London.
helping word **have**

A Choose the right word from the pair above to fill each space.

1 **has** **have**
He can't run because he ____ a bad leg.

2 **was** **were**
The boy ____ afraid of the bull.

3 **was** **were**
Several cows ____ grazing in the field.

4 **did** **done**
They have ____ everything I asked them to do.

5 **is** **are**
James ____ a very kind boy.

6 **saw** **seen**
I have never ____ an eclipse of the sun.

B Write the word which will fill each gap.

1 **saw** **seen**
Three people ____ the accident.

2 **did** **done**
Sarah ____ her best to tidy the garage.

3 **is** **are**
The book ____ kept on the shelf.

4 **did** **done**
Philip rested when he had ____ his work.

5 **saw** **seen**
It is the biggest trout I have ____ .

6 **is** **are**
The books ____ kept on the shelf.

Words with more than one meaning

Some words have more than one meaning.

Examples
The brown **bear** climbed the tree.
Sandra could hardly **bear** the pain.

bark	light
blow	match
chest	ring
fair	shed
kind	watch

Use the words in the list on the left to fill the spaces in the sentences. The same word must be used for each pair of sentences.

1   The lawn mower is kept in the garden ____ .
    Many trees ____ their leaves in the autumn.

2   The ____ woman put £1 in the collecting box.
    This is a different ____ of toffee.

3   It is time to ____ the school bell.
    The wedding ____ was made of solid gold.

4   The oak tree has a rough ____ .
    The dog began to ____ when the children teased him.

5   Much damage is done when high winds ____ .
    A ____ on the head knocked the boxer out.

6   Sara has very ____ hair.
    There were many amusements at the ____ .

7   My new ____ keeps very good time.
    We did not ____ television last night.

8   The parcel was as ____ as a feather.
    The bedside lamp gave out lots of ____ .

9   There was a big crowd at the football ____ .
    Grandad struck a ____ and lit his pipe.

10 James has a cold on his ____ .
    The tools are kept in a big wooden ____ .

Using capital letters

Capital letters are used:

to begin a sentence	**A**lways start a sentence with a capital letter.
for the names of people and pets	**G**eorge, **J**ennifer, **F**luffy, **P**ongo Also for **M**r., **M**rs., **D**r.
for the names of places, rivers, mountains and so on	**B**ristol, **T**hames, **S**nowdon, **A**tlantic
for addresses	29 **S**outh **R**oad, **B**arnsdale, **BA**12 3**QT**.
for the names of the days of the week	**M**onday, **W**ednesday, **S**aturday
for the word I	**I** did my best but **I** failed.

Copy these sentences, using capital letters where they are needed.

1   henry chaplin lives in hastings.

2   the national gallery has some beautiful paintings.

3   david and i are going to london for a day.

4   we hope to go next friday.

5   the highest mountain in wales is snowdon.

6   canterbury is in kent.

7   a new shop has opened in bond street.

8   my mother and i are going to australia in july.

9   colin has a pet dog named pepper.

10   we paid a visit to mr. and mrs. reeve.

Raman meets the rocking-horse

Raman asked his mother after school if he could go home and play with Jock. She said, "Yes," and she would come and fetch him at half-past five. She wore a long, flowing sari, and Jock thought she was very beautiful.

"She's an Indian princess," he thought. "I'll ride to her rescue if she's in danger."

When they reached Jock's house, Jock took Raman into the basement room, and went up to the horse and patted his neck.

"What's he called?" asked Raman, gazing at the horse with admiration.

"I don't know yet," answered Jock and added quickly: "At least I do, but his name's a secret. He only allows *me* to call him by it."

This was not quite true, as Jock hadn't yet invented a name for him, but he knew that he would sometime.

"He's wonderful," breathed Raman. "Can I have a ride?"

"Well, he doesn't like strangers much," answered Jock. "I'll ride him first so that he can look at you and get used to you."

The Rocking-Horse   Rosemary Manning

1   At what time of day did Raman go to play with Jock?
2   What is a **sari**?
3   What is the difference between **gazing** and **looking**?
4   Why did Jock think of Raman's mother as a princess?
5   In what part of the house was the rocking-horse kept?
6   What reason did Jock give Raman for not telling him the horse's name?
7   What was Jock's real reason for not telling him?
8   What reason did Jock give Raman for having the first ride himself?

Here and hear/There and their

here
means **in this place**.

I left the bag **here** five minutes ago.

hear
You **hear** with your ears.

We could **hear** the thrushes singing.

there
means **in that place**.

He lives over **there**.

their
means **belonging to them**.

The boys played with **their** football.

A Write **here** or **hear** in each space.

1 Will you stay ____ till I come back?

2 Ann did not ____ her mother calling her.

3 We could ____ someone snoring in the next room.

4 ____ is the ball you were looking for.

5 Would you like to live ____?

6 Deaf people cannot ____ .

B Write **there** or **their** in each space.

1 The children gave ____ dog a bath.

2 I waited ____ for nearly an hour.

3 ____ are a hundred pence in a pound.

4 Is ____ room for me to sit down?

5 The two boys went to the show with ____ cousin.

6 I saw patches of clover here and ____ on the lawn.

7 He said he left the parcel ____ and now it's gone.

8 We looked here, ____ , and everywhere.

9 ____ excuse for being late was ridiculous.

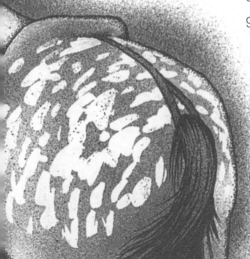

Plurals

Singular means **one**.

Plural means **more than one**.

Singular	Plural
boy	boys
glass	glasses
daisy	daisies
leaf	leaves

leaf

leaves

A Add **-s** to each word to form the plural.

1	bird	4	farmer	7	river
2	cook	5	tree	8	coat
3	head	6	chair		

B Add **-es** to each word to form the plural.

1	bush	4	brush	7	church
2	bunch	5	box	8	match
3	coach	6	dish		

C Change **y** to **i** and add **-es**.

1	fly	4	berry	7	city
2	pony	5	story	8	penny
3	baby	6	lady		

D Change **f** to **v** and add **-es**.

1	elf	4	half	7	wolf
2	shelf	5	calf	8	sheaf
3	loaf	6	leaf		

E Copy these sentences, making each noun in bold type plural.

Example   1   They fed the calves on milk.

1   They fed the **calf** on milk.

2   The **butcher** sharpened the **knife**.

3   The **baker** put the burnt **loaf** on the **shelf**.

4   The **gardener** trimmed the **bush**.

5   The **elf** stitched the **shoe**.

6   The **leaf** fell from the **tree**.

7   The **fly** buzzed round the **baby**.

8   The **girl** put the **penny** in the **box**.

Verbs adding -ed and -ing

When we add **-ed** or **-ing** to each of the words in this list we double the last letter.

nod
nodded
nodding

hum
hummed
humming

drop
dropped
dropping

grin
grinned
grinning

A Add **-ing** to each word, first doubling the last letter.

1	peg	6	skim
2	chat	7	drop
3	rob	8	skid
4	stab	9	drag
5	hum	10	slip

B Add **-ed** to each word, first doubling the last letter.

1	snap	6	dip
2	grin	7	trim
3	lap	8	grab
4	rub	9	slam
5	nod	10	drip

C Fill each space with the right verb.

1 Water was ____ from a hole in the can.

2 The car ____ on the wet road and crashed.

3 Joy ____ a merry tune as she went along.

4 Mum ____ the wet clothes on the line.

5 The rude boy ____ the door as he went out.

6 Alan ____ on a banana skin and hurt his leg.

7 The gardener was busy ____ the hedge.

8 A lovely white kitten was ____ a saucer of milk.

The end stops

A **full stop** is put at the end of every statement.

Example
I hung my coat on the coat-hanger.

A **question mark** is put at the end of every question.

Example
Did you hang your coat on the coat-hanger?

An **exclamation mark** is put at the end of every shouted command.

Example
Put that down at once!

Full stops, question marks and exclamation marks are all **end stops**.

A   Copy each sentence. Put a full stop, a question mark or an exclamation mark at the end of each.

1   The bushy tail of a fox is called a brush

2   A camel can go for days without water

3   Have you visited the Tower of London

4   The Nile is a long river in Africa

5   Don't you dare do that

6   Will you call for me in the morning

7   Our school starts at nine o'clock

8   Did you post the letter I gave you

9   Beavers can gnaw through big trees

10   Put that down immediately

11   Are you sorry you are leaving Liverpool

12   Just go away

B   Write two statements, two questions and two commands. Remember to use the correct end stop.

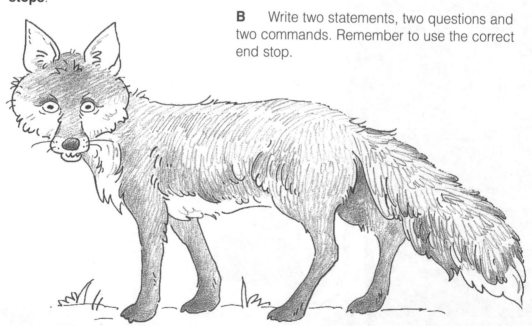

Forming nouns

Some nouns are formed by adding **-ness** to words.

sad	sadness
slow	slowness
deaf	deafness
stout	stoutness

When **-ness** is added to words ending with **y**, the **y** is changed to **i**.

steady	steadiness
shabby	shabbiness
sleepy	sleepiness

A Add **-ness** to these words.

1	glad	6	greedy	11	sore
2	stale	7	lame	12	sad
3	quick	8	blind	13	giddy
4	tired	9	rough	14	wicked
5	loud	10	fresh	15	good

B Fill each space with the noun formed from the word in bold type.

1 Jennie thanked her teacher for her ___ . **kind**

2 The wolves started to howl as ___ fell. **dark**

3 Winter often brings much ___ . **ill**

4 It is ___ to speed on busy roads. **mad**

5 The wood was two centimetres in ___ . **thick**

6 The old man was suffering from ___ . **giddy**

7 We were surprised at the ___ of the squirrels. **tame**

8 The man's ___ was caused by an explosion. **deaf**

9 Mrs. Platt scolded Ben for his ___ . **lazy**

10 Chandra was dazzled by the ___ of the sun. **bright**

Some useful finds

Just then the rubbish dump came into sight, and they started
to run towards it. It was a flattish hill of ashes and cinders,
mixed with old tyres and broken furniture.

James and Jenny began to climb over this hill of rubbish,
exclaiming every time they found a treasure. Penny followed,
not liking the dust that rose under her feet, and the crunch of
the cinders, but was as pleased as the others when she found a
big bundle of paper with one side plain.

"Drawing paper!" she called out. "Scribbling paper!
Sheets and sheets and sheets. We can make it pretty, and paper
the whole of the dolls' house. We can play schools, too."

"A chain" said James, clanking it joyfully. "A strong,
useful chain. We can play at prisons and I'll chain you up."

The Bicycle Wheel   Ruth Ainsworth

1   What four things did the rubbish dump consist
    of?
2   Explain what is meant by the word **treasure** in
    this passage.
3   What did James and Jenny do every time they
    found a treasure?
4   What two things did Penny not like about the
    dump?
5   What made Penny pleased when she looked
    through the dump?
6   What three things did Penny want to do with the
    paper?
7   What is the difference between **shaking** a chain
    and **clanking** it?
8   James used two adjectives to describe the
    chain. What are they?
9   What did he suggest they did with it?
10 How do you think the children felt as they
    climbed over the dump?

Adjectives describing words

Adjectives can be formed by adding **-y** to some words.

rust	rusty
greed	greedy
wealth	wealthy
storm	stormy

When **-y** is added to some words the last letter of the word is doubled.

sun	sunny
fog	foggy
skin	skinny
fur	furry
bag	baggy

When **-y** is added to a word ending with **e** this letter is dropped.

noise	noisy
smoke	smoky
ease	easy
shade	shady
stone	stony

A What are the missing words?

1 Hands covered with dirt   ____ hands

2 A day of strong winds   a ____ day

3 A mountain with many rocks   a ____ mountain

4 A beach covered with sand   a ____ beach

5 A table covered with dust   a ____ table

6 A chest covered with hair   a ____ chest

7 Hair which has curls   ____ hair

8 Food which has a lot of salt ____ food

9 A sky with many clouds   a ____ sky

10 A girl who has lots of luck a ____ girl

B What are the missing adjectives?

1 a ____ day   **sun**

2 an ____ exercise **ease**

3 a ____ hand   **skin**

4 a ____ animal   **fur**

5 a ____ chimney   **smoke**

6 a ____ class   **noise**

7 ____ trousers   **bag**

8 a ____ tree   **shade**

9 a ____ path   **stone**

10 a ____ night   **fog**

11 a ____ line   **wave**

12 a ____ joke   **fun**

13 a ____ face   **spot**

14 a ____ pupil   **laze**

15 a ____ lane   **mud**

Verbs adding -es and -ed

When **-es** or **-ed** is added to a verb ending with **y**, this letter is first changed to **i**.

I **try** hard.

He **tries** hard.

She **tried** hard.

A   Copy and fill in the missing letters.

1	try	. . . es	6	dirty	. . . . . es
2	cry	. . . ed	7	copy	. . . . ed
3	dry	. . . ed	8	empty	. . . . . es
4	fry	. . . es	9	hurry	. . . . . ed
5	spy	. . . ed	10	carry	. . . . . es

B   Finish each sentence by using the right form of the verb in bold type, adding **-es** or **-ed** as needed.

1   Rushkana is . . . . every morning that she will miss the bus.   **worry**

2   Every day Ann . . . . . . sums from Soraya.   **copy**

3   She . . . . . because she had cut her knee.   **cry**

4   Although we . . . . to the station we missed the train.   **hurry**

5   Again and again the little spider . . . . . to climb up the thread.   **try**

6   David . . . . his books to school in a satchel.   **carry**

7   Every time she washes her hands she . . . . . them well.   **dry**

8   Yesterday the dustmen . . . . all the bins in our street.   **empty**

9   I . . . . . an owl up the church tower.   **spy**

10   My mother says that she . . . . . . people with curly hair.   **envy**

Same sound — different meaning

Some words have the same sound as other words, but they are different in spelling and meaning.

Look at these four pairs of words.

bare   A **bare** tree has no leaves.

bear   The polar **bear** is a very big animal.

dear   The dress was too **dear** so she did not buy it.
Jane is a very **dear** friend of mine.

deer   A **deer** is a graceful animal.

fair   **Fair** hair is light in colour.
We had fun at the **fair**.

fare   The bus conductor asked me for my **fare**.

heel   The back part of your foot is called the **heel**.

heal   To **heal** people means to make them well.

Choose the correct word from the pair above to complete each sentence.

1 **fair**   **fare**
The bus ____ to school is fifty pence.

2 **heel**   **heal**
The cut on your finger will soon ____ .

3 **bear**   **bare**
The big brown ____ sat up and begged.

4 **heel**   **heal**
The ____ of the woman's shoe came right off.

5 **fair**   **fare**
Peter won a coconut at the ____ .

6 **bear**   **bare**
Many trees are ____ in winter.

7 **dear**   **deer**
We saw ten ____ in the park.

dear
dear
de—r
deer
deer

Punctuation

Putting full stops, commas, question marks, etc., in sentences is called **punctuation**.

1 A full stop is used to end a sentence which makes a statement.

Example *Gold is mined in South Africa.*

2 A question mark is used to end a sentence which asks a question.

Example *How many days are there in a week?*

3 An exclamation mark is used after a word or a sentence which is spoken excitedly, and after shouted commands.

Example *Run! The tide's coming in fast!*

4 Commas are used:

a to separate the name of a person directly spoken to from the rest of the sentence.

Examples *Richard, have you locked the door?*
Have you locked the door, Richard?

b to separate words in a list when **and** or **or** is used to separate the last two words only.

Example *Gold, iron, silver and lead are all metals.*

c after words like **well**, **oh**, **yes**, **no** and **now** when they begin a sentence.

Example *Well, I warned you not to do it.*

d to set off the word **please** at the end of a sentence.

Example *Have you the right time, please?*

Insert punctuation marks in these sentences.

1 Have you ever spent a holiday abroad

2 Yes I went to Spain last summer

3 Please lock up before you go Philip

4 Jennifer have you finished your homework

5 Cyprus Corsica Malta Elba and Sicily are all islands

Similars

A **wealthy** man
A **rich** man

The words **wealthy** and **rich** have much the same meaning.

Learn the list of similars before answering the questions.

collect	gather
difficult	hard
pile	heap
commence	begin
hasten	hurry
peril	danger
weeping	crying
drowsy	sleepy
naked	bare
plucky	brave

A   Write a simpler word in place of each word in bold type.

1   The concert will **commence** at 7 o'clock.

2   Janine found the sum very **difficult**.

3   The ship was in great **peril**.

4   A **pile** of stones lay outside the school.

5   The **plucky** sailor saved the boy's life.

6   At the funeral several women were **weeping**.

7   Sitting near a big fire makes one **drowsy**.

8   The sun shone on the swimmer's **naked** back.

B   In each group below select the word which is similar in meaning to the word in bold type.

1   **drowsy**

lively
quick
active
sleepy

2   **hasten**

fix
hurry
work
play

3   **collect**

give
spend
gather
climb

4   **difficult**

clever
easy
hard
simple

5   **peril**

danger
length
safety
depth

6   **plucky**

silly
brave
short
noisy

7   **assist**

help
coax
hinder
wait

8   **halt**

hurry
linger
run
stop

9   **feeble**

loving
weak
silly
famous

Magic balloons

You will need two balloons, a little sugar and a sheet of paper torn into small pieces.

1   Blow up the balloons. You may need an adult to help you do this. Tie the end of each balloon into a firm knot.

2   Now rub each balloon hard against your sweater. The trick works best if the sweater you are wearing is made of wool.

3   Hold one balloon just above the torn pieces of paper. What happens? Then try holding a balloon just above some sugar.

The balloons pick up the torn up paper and sugar, as if by magic.

Rubbing a balloon against wool charges it with static electricity. This gives the balloon enough magnetic power to pick up very light things, like the paper and sugar. It also makes the paper and sugar stick to the balloon.

Most things contain static electricity. You cannot see it, but you can rub it off one thing and on to another, making it static.

My First Science Book   Angela Wilkes

1   What can you make the balloons do after you have rubbed them against a wool sweater?
2   What is making the balloons pick up the paper and sugar?
3   Why are paper and sugar good things to use in the experiment?
4   We are seeing an **invisible** force at work in this experiment. What does **invisible** mean?
5   **Magic** balloons? True or false? Explain.
6   Find a word in the passage that begins with a silent l
7   Find a word in the passage that rhymes with **try**.
8   Find three words in the passage that end with **-ic**.

Fun with words

In each column opposite there are two pairs of words and one odd word.

You have to find the word which will make up the third pair.

Look at the first pair of words in **A**: **ear   hear**

The second word is made by adding the letter **h** to the beginning of the first word.

Look at the second pair:
at   hat

The second word is again formed by writing **h** before the first word.

To find the missing word write **h** before the odd word.

Example   **arm   harm**

A   Now find the other missing words. In every column a different letter must be added.

1   ear   hear   2   all   ball   3   ark   park
     at   hat   eat   beat   ink   pink
     arm   ____   oil   ____   lay   ____

4   ill   mill   5   old   gold
     ask   mask   lad   glad
     other   ____   race   ____

B   In each line below the same letter ends the first word and begins the second. Write the ten pairs of words.

Example   sat   tea

1   sa .   . ea
2   be .   . og
3   sh .   . gg
4   bi .   . un
5   wa .   . ly
6   pos .   . rap
7   fil .   . ift
8   goo .   . oor
9   hea .   . ich
10   hel .   . lay

C   Test your word power. Can you supply the missing letters? All the words end in **-ic**.

1   When the chain was shaken, it made a me _ _ _ _ ic noise.

2   My parents were fr _ _ _ ic with worry when I was late home.

3   Keep calm and don't pa _ ic.

4   How can you charge a balloon with st _ _ ic electricity?

5   Wash that cut carefully or it will turn se _ _ ic.

Showing ownership

I like Simon's new puppy.

The **'s** in Simon's shows that the puppy **belongs** to Simon. It is **his**. He **owns** it.

A Copy these in your book, putting in the **'** before the **s**.

1 the robin s breast
2 the sailor s cap
3 the horse s mane
4 the rabbit s tail
5 the old man s beard
6 the cashier s till
7 the lady s handbag
8 the sheep s wool
9 the Queen s crown
10 the dog s collar

the kite which belongs to Paul
(long way)

Paul's kite   *(short way)*

B Write these the short way.

1 the book belonging to Mary
2 the bat which belongs to Peter
3 the ribbon belonging to Ann
4 the watch which belongs to Dad
5 the ring which belongs to Mum

the wool of the sheep
(long way)

the sheep's wool   *(short way)*

C Write these the short way.

1 the fur of the cat
2 the den of the lion
3 the beak of the blackbird
4 the ears of the donkey
5 the horns of the cow

Opposites using un

safe   **unsafe**

Some words are given an opposite meaning by writing **un** before them.

Look at the words above the pictures.

A Form the opposites of these words by using **un**.

1	happy	5	do	9	roll
2	willing	6	screw	10	real
3	paid	7	tie	11	safe
4	seen	8	wise	12	steady

B Choose any six of the words you have made and use them in sentences of your own.

C Copy these sentences, adding **un** to the words in bold type to give them an opposite meaning.

1 The new road is **finished**.

2 The doctor said that Martin was very **healthy**.

3 The pears were **ripe**.

4 The referee was **fair** in what he said.

5 Janine was **kind** to animals.

6 Dad could not **lock** the car.

7 The gym had an **even** floor.

8 The man was **known** to the police.

Alphabetical order

Look at the alphabet.

**abcd
efgh
ijklm
nopq
rstuv
wxyz**

A

1 Write the third letter of the alphabet.

2 Which letter is last but one?

3 Which letter comes between **j** and **l**?

4 What are the missing letters?
g h . j k . m n o . q

B Write each group of words in **a-b-c** or alphabetical order. Look at the first letter of each word.

1	head	2	look	3	green
	train		ready		water
	before		winter		cross
	food		another		idea
	also		small		pull

4	paint	5	please
	teach		answer
	little		mountain
	heart		young
	alone		under

C In each group below all the words are in alphabetical order except one. Write the odd word in each group.

Example   Group 1   bicycle

1	night	2	army	3	early
	orange		bread		dress
	pretty		colour		figure
	queen		letter		garden
	bicycle		doctor		house

4	kitchen	5	beauty
	length		ground
	window		middle
	mouse		season
	north		heavy

Short forms

You have learnt how to join two words, one of which is **not**.

is not	isn't
was not	wasn't
does not	doesn't
has not	hasn't

Notice that the **'** stands for the **o** which is left out.

We can also join **is** to another word in this way.

he is	he's
she is	she's
it is	it's
who is	who's
that is	that's
what is	what's
where is	where's
there is	there's

Remember that the **'** stands for the **i** which is left out.

Write these sentences, joining the two words in bold type in each.

1   Brian says **he is** too busy to play.

2   I think **that is** a lovely dress.

3   Clare is tall, and **she is** pretty, too.

4   Thank goodness **it is** a fine day.

5   We can't work when **there is** a noise in the room.

6   I can guess **what is** in the box.

7   I wonder **who is** going to the party tonight.

8   **It is** not raining now.

9   Roger **does not** like going to town.

10 The pears **are not** quite ripe.

Lone Dog

I'm a lean dog, a keen dog, a wild dog and lone,
I'm a rough dog, a tough dog, hunting on my own!
I'm a bad dog, a mad dog, teasing silly sheep;
I love to sit and bay at the moon and keep fat souls from sleep.

I'll never be a lap dog, licking dirty feet,
A sleek dog, a meek dog, cringing for my meat.
Not for me the fireside, the well-filled plate,
But shut the door and sharp stone and cuff and kick and hate.

Not for me the other dogs, running by my side,
Some have run a short while, but none of them would bide.
O mine is still the lone trail, the hard trail, the best,
Wide wind and wild stars and the hunger of the quest.

Irene McLeod

A

1   Which word in the first verse rhymes with **lone**?

2   Which word in the first line rhymes with **lean**?

3   Find a pair of words which rhyme in the third
line.

4   Make a list of three pairs of words which rhyme
in the second verse.

5   Which word in the third verse rhymes with **best**?

B   How does the dog feel about being a "lone
dog"?
Choose five words from the list below that you
feel describe his feelings best. (Remember to
use a dictionary to check the meanings of the
words.)

sad	hungry	defiant
proud	resolute	jealous
lonely	independent	pathetic
happy	bitter	depressed

Noises of animals

I bark

I crow

I cluck

I bleat

I mew

I bray

I moo

I quack

A Write the noise words.

1 sheep ____
2 ducks ____
3 dogs ____
4 cows ____

5 donkeys ____
6 cockerels ____
7 hens ____
8 cats ____

B Fill each space with the name of the creature or the name of the noise it makes.

1 The dog was ____ at a squirrel.

2 We heard the cows ____ in the meadow.

3 The loud braying of a ____ frightened the children.

4 The cat was ____ because she had hurt her paw.

5 The ____ bleated as the dog rounded them up.

6 The boys were up before the ____ started crowing.

7 Robert's brown ____ clucked after laying an egg.

8 The ____ quacked as it came towards me.

Verbs

I **like** apples.

Sally **likes** apples.

We both **like** apples.

I, you, we, they	**he, she, it**
do	does
go	goes
put	puts
run	runs
pull	pulls
play	plays
say	says
try	tries
carry	carries
hurry	hurries

A   Copy and fill in the missing verb.

1   they ____   **go   goes**

2   I ____   **try   tries**

3   he ____   **pull   pulls**

4   you ____   **say   says**

5   we ____   **do   does**

6   she ____   **put   puts**

7   you ____   **hurry   hurries**

8   it ____   **run   runs**

9   I ____   **carry   carries**

10   they ____   **play   plays**

B   Write the verb from the list on the left which will fill each space correctly.

1   The children ____ football every day.

2   Mr. Gold ____ his umbrella on his arm.

3   Judith ____ her knitting by the fire.

4   We ____ to school five days a week.

5   Peter ____ his prayers every night.

6   I will catch the bus if I ____ .

7   Our cat always ____ after a mouse.

8   Zena ____ hard to write a good letter.

C   Write sentences of your own showing how each of these words can be used.

1   make   makes   4   think   thinks

2   eat   eats   5   walk   walks

3   read   reads   6   learn   learns

Writing letters

A   Read the letter which Tom Weller wrote to his friend Ben Baxter inviting him to his birthday party. Tom's mother showed him how to arrange the letter and how to address the envelope.

Notice the postcode HD24 3PX. Always show the postcode in the last line of your address.

Pretend you are Ben Baxter and that you have just had this letter from Tom.

Write a letter to him thanking him for his kind invitation and telling him that you will be delighted to come.

Draw an envelope and address it to Tom. You will find his address at the top of his letter.

B   Pretend that you have been to Tom's party. Write a letter to another friend who was not there telling him how much you enjoyed yourself. Say what you had to eat, what games you played and what fireworks you saw.

Draw an envelope and address it to your friend.

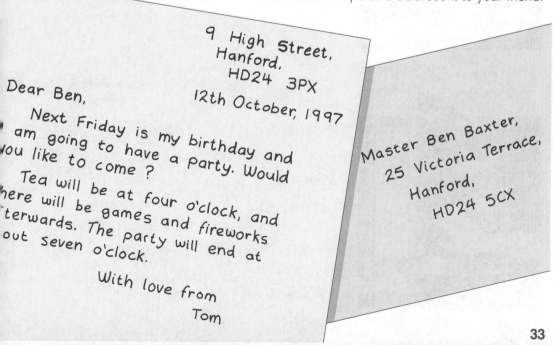

9 High Street,
Hanford,
HD24 3PX
12th October, 1997

Dear Ben,
    Next Friday is my birthday and
am going to have a party. Would
you like to come ?
    Tea will be at four o'clock, and
there will be games and fireworks
afterwards. The party will end at
about seven o'clock.
        With love from
                Tom

Master Ben Baxter,
25 Victoria Terrace,
Hanford,
HD24 5CX

Sounds

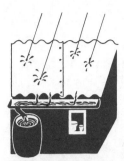

patter

toot

ringing

beat

clatter

tick

chinking

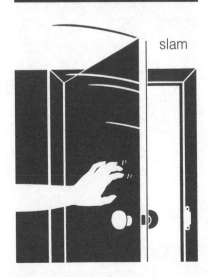
slam

A Write the name of each sound.

1 the ＿＿ of dishes

2 the ＿＿ of a drum

3 the ＿＿ of bells

4 the ＿＿ of a clock

5 the ＿＿ of a door

6 the ＿＿ of a horn

7 the ＿＿ of coins

8 the ＿＿ of raindrops

B Write the **sound** word which suits each sentence.

1 The ＿＿ of raindrops on the window awakened the children.

2 We heard the ＿＿ of drums as the soldiers drew near.

3 The room was so quiet that we could hear the ＿＿ of the clock.

4 I could hear the ＿＿ of coins in his pocket.

5 From the kitchen came the ＿＿ of dishes.

6 With a ＿＿ of the door Jonathan left the room in a bad temper.

7 The car went past with a ＿＿ of the horn.

8 Every Sunday the ＿＿ of church bells could be heard in the village.

Collections

A number of **sheep** together is called a **flock**.

A number of **tools** together is called a **set**.

a herd of cows
a litter of puppies
a galaxy of stars
a flock of sheep
a gang of thieves
a swarm of bees
a shoal of fish
a pair of shoes
a flight of steps
a bunch of grapes
a hand of bananas
a suit of clothes
a chest of drawers
a crowd of people
a pack of wolves
a pack of cards
a gaggle of geese
a set of tools
a host of angels

A Write the missing words. You will find them in the list on the left.

1 a ___ of people   6 a flight of ___

2 a ___ of wolves   7 a chest of ___

3 a ___ of grapes   8 a shoal of ___

4 a ___ of shoes   9 a herd of ___

5 a ___ of clothes   10 a flock of ___

B Write the word which will fill each gap.

1 A ___ of steps led to the cabin.

2 A ___ of geese waddled across the yard.

3 Our milk comes from a ___ of Jersey cows.

4 A pack of ___ went hunting in the forest.

5 A ___ of fish swam past our boat.

6 A ___ of people gathered to welcome the Prince.

7 The clothes were kept in an old ___ of drawers.

8 She bought a new ___ of shoes for the wedding.

9 Dad gave his old ___ of clothes to a jumble sale.

10 A ___ of bees settled on Matthew's head and shoulders.

Tom Thumb

The woodman took his family into a very thick wood where they could not see one another ten paces off. The woodman began to cut some wood, and the children to gather up the sticks and to make them into bundles. Their father and mother, seeing them all so busy, crept away from them bit by bit, and then all at once ran away through the bushes.

When the children saw that they had been left alone they started to cry loudly. Tom Thumb let them cry, for he had taken care to drop all along the road the little white stones he had in his pockets.

Then he said to them, "Do not be afraid, brothers. Father and Mother have left us here, but I will take you home again; only follow me."

They followed him, and he brought them home through the wood by the same road as they had come.

Tales from Perrault

1 Where did the woodman take his family?
2 What did he do when they got there?
3 How did the children help their father?
4 What did the father and mother do when the children were busy?
5 Why did the children start to cry?
6 Why did Tom let them cry?
7 What had Tom done on the way to the wood?
8 How was Tom able to take his brothers home again?

Group names

The **robin** is a **bird**. So is the **sparrow** and so is the **thrush**.

They all belong to the same **group**. They are all **birds**.

animals
flowers
dogs
fruits
colours
insects
days
tools
fish
trees

A   Use a group name from the list on the left to finish each sentence.

1   Oak, ash, birch and elm are all ____ .

2   Terrier, corgi, spaniel and collie are all ____ .

3   Hammer, saw, pincers and chisel are all ____ .

4   Monday, Thursday, Friday and Tuesday are all ____ .

5   Herring, cod, hake and haddock are all ____ .

6   Fly, wasp, bee and gnat are all ____ .

7   Lion, tiger, bear and wolf are all ____ .

8   Red, blue, yellow and green are all ____ .

9   Rose, lily, tulip and crocus are all ____ .

10   Pear, apple, plum and banana are all ____ .

B   In each column below there is one word which does not belong to the same group as the others.
Write the odd word.

1		2		3	
willow		blue		apple	
oak		bright		orange	
birch		black		turnip	
daffodil		yellow		lemon	
beech		green		pear	

4		5		6	
cow		Christmas		violet	
goat		Friday		dandelion	
sheep		Wednesday		bluebell	
moth		Monday		mushroom	
horse		Thursday		snowdrop	

People who work

A   Use the words in the list on the left to name each person. Number your words 1 to 8 as in the pictures.

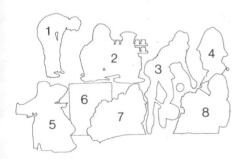

potter	fishmonger
gardener	hairdresser
farmer	flight attendant
teacher	police officer
porter	window cleaner
guard	tennis player
sailor	fire fighter
soldier	

B   Write the missing words. The list on the left will help you.

1   I asked the ____ when the plane was going to land.

2   The ____ had some fine fillets of hake.

3   The ____ is giving a maths lesson.

4   The ____ wheeled Martin's trunk to the luggage van.

5   Jane has gone to the ____ to have her hair cut.

6   The ____ blew the whistle and the train moved off.

7   The ____ went aboard the battleship.

8   We watched the ____ cutting the hay.

9   The ____ on sentry duty carried a rifle.

10   A big crowd saw the ____ rescue the boy from the burning house.

The doers of actions

The person who **teaches** you
is your **teacher**.
Teach is the action.
Teacher is the **doer** of the
action.

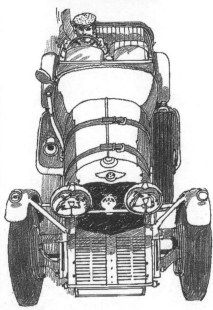

A Add **-er** to each of these verbs to make
the name of a doer.

1	help	4	bowl	7	clean
2	build	5	read	8	dream
3	lead	6	paint	9	sing

B Before adding **-er** to these words, double
the last letter.

1	run	4	win	7	trap
2	rob	5	drum	8	travel
3	shop	6	swim	9	begin

C Drop the **e** when you add **-er** to these
words.

1	ride	3	drive	5	strike
2	dance	4	explore	6	write

D Change **y** to **i** before adding **-er**.

1 carry   2 supply

E Write the words which fill the spaces.

1 Andrew was a strong ____ .   **swim**

2 The ____ could not keep in step with his
partner.   **dance**

3 Louise is a very quick ____ .   **read**

4 The ____ was given a gold medal.   **win**

5 He has been a ____ with the band for ten
years.   **drum**

6 The ____ sent two parcels to the
school.   **supply**

7 Our ____ keeps the school very tidy.   **clean**

8 A policeman stopped the ____ of the sports
car.   **drive**

39

Male and female

A **boy** is a **he**, or a **male**.
A **man** is a **he**, or a **male**.

A **girl** is a **she**, or a **female**.
A **woman** is a **she**, or a **female**.

Male	Female
actor	actress
cockerel	hen
dog	bitch
gander	goose
grandfather	grandmother
duke	duchess
prince	princess
son	daughter
tiger	tigress
waiter	waitress
uncle	aunt
nephew	niece
husband	wife
king	queen
ram	ewe
stallion	mare
bull	cow

A   Copy this column, then write the missing words.

	Male	Female
1	___	princess
2	grandfather	___
3	___	daughter
4	waiter	___
5	gander	___
6	___	bitch
7	___	tigress
8	___	actress
9	cockerel	___
10	___	duchess

B   Change **male** words to **female**, and **female** to **male**.

1   The waitress took our order and left.

2   The actor tripped over the scenery and fell on his face.

3   The goose hissed at the children.

4   Her husband was at work.

5   The teacher's son was very ill.

6   The hunter shot the huge tiger.

7   The old hen scratched in the earth for worms.

8   In the evening the prince walked in the garden.

9   I gave my nephew £10.

10   My daughter is afraid of cows.

Animals

A Write the names of these animals.

B Write the name of the animal which will complete each sentence. You will find them in the list on the left.

1   The ____ is covered with sharp spines and can roll itself into a ball when attacked.

2   The ____ has a long trunk and strong tusks.

3   The ____ has a hump on its back and can carry people and goods across the desert.

4   The ____ has a spotted skin and a very long neck.

5   The ____ has a bushy tail which curls over its back.

6   The ____ is a cunning animal which steals chickens.

7   The ____ is called the King of Beasts. Its loud roar frightens many animals.

8   The ____ is a stubborn animal with very long ears. It is sometimes called an ass.

bear   giraffe
fox   hedgehog
lion   elephant
camel   kangaroo
donkey   squirrel

9   The ____ has strong hind legs which enable it to move forward in great leaps.

10 A ____ has a shaggy coat and strong claws. It can hug a person to death.

The fox and the goat

While reaching down to drink the water in a well one day, a fox fell in. Try as he would, he could not get out again because the walls of the well were too high.

Not long after, a goat came along. Seeing the fox down there, he asked him the reason why.

"I am enjoying the cool, pure water," replied the fox. "Wouldn't you like to jump down and taste it?"

Without stopping to think, the foolish old goat jumped down. No sooner had he reached the bottom than the cunning old fox leaped on to his back and scrambled to the top.

Looking down at the unhappy goat, the fox laughed and said, "Next time, friend goat, be sure to look before you leap."

Aesop's Fables

1   What did the fox have to do before he could drink the water in the well?
2   What happened to him while he was doing this?
3   Why could he not get out of the well?
4   What did the goat ask the fox?
5   What was the answer given by the fox?
6   What did the goat do when the fox asked him to try the water?
7   How did the fox get to the top again?
8   What did he tell the goat to do the next time?

Adverbs

Andrew tiptoed **quietly** from the room.

The word **quietly** tells us how he left the room.

This word is formed by adding **-ly** to quiet.

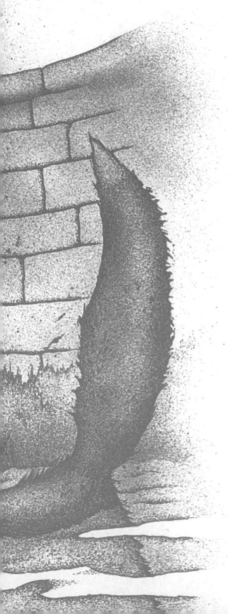

A Add **-ly** to each of these words.

quick	safe	kind
calm	neat	fond
sad	quiet	proud

B When **-ly** is added to words ending with **y**, this letter is first changed to **i**.

Examples

clumsy	clumsily
hasty	hastily

Add **-ly** to these words.

easy	lucky	greedy
busy	heavy	hungry
sleepy	angry	weary
noisy	steady	thirsty

C The word which fills each space below is formed by adding **-ly** to the word in bold type. Write the nine words.

1 The flames spread so ____ that the house was soon burnt to the ground. **quick**

2 All the boys were working ____ . **busy**

3 The ship arrived ____ after a stormy voyage. **safe**

4 The snail crept ____ along the garden path. **slow**

5 The old man nodded his head ____ . **sleepy**

6 It is raining too ____ for you to go out. **heavy**

7 The young mother looked ____ at her baby. **proud**

8 Jo wrote the letter very ____ . **neat**

9 Zek jumped over the wall quite ____ . **easy**

43

Opposites change of word

Look at this list of opposites, then answer the questions.

back	front
buy	sell
glad	sorry
bitter	sweet
dark	light
long	short
poor	rich
break	mend
fast	slow
noisy	quiet

A Use the opposite of the word in bold type to fill each space.

Example a fast train **slow**

1 to ___ a rabbit **buy**

2 a ___ room **dark**

3 a ___ seat **back**

4 a ___ story **long**

5 a ___ orange **sweet**

6 a ___ street **quiet**

7 a ___ man **poor**

8 to ___ a toy **break**

9 to be ___ **glad**

B Fill each gap with the opposite of the word in bold type.

1 If you ___ your arm it will take about six weeks to **mend**.

2 We are going to paint the **front** and the ___ of our house.

3 He was ___ when his cousin came but **sorry** when he left.

4 Uncle will **sell** his old car and ___ a new one.

5 He tied the ___ length of cord to the **long** one.

6 The children were **quiet** in school but very ___ outside.

7 Ten years ago he was ___. Now he is very **rich**.

8 He wore a **dark** grey suit and a ___ grey hat.

9 The clock was five minutes **fast** yesterday but it is ___ today.

Group names

An apple is
a **fruit**.

A cabbage is
a **vegetable**.

A rose is
a **flower**.

A teddy bear is
a **toy**.

bird
fish
toy
tree
tool
fruit
flower
insect
animal
vegetable

A Write the group name for each of these
objects. Use the list on the left to help you.

1 A doll is a ___ .
2 A peach is a ___ .
3 A herring is a ___ .
4 An oak is a ___ .
5 A tiger is an ___ .
6 A wasp is an ___ .
7 A turnip is a ___ .
8 A crocus is a ___ .
9 A sparrow is a ___ .
10 A hammer is a ___ .

B Draw four columns in your book, like
these. Then put the words below in their correct
columns.

Fruits	Fishes	Vegetables	Tools
parsnip	cabbage	trowel	plum
rake	lemon	mackerel	salmon
orange	plaice	beetroot	onion
carrot	spade	banana	hatchet
herring	apricot	spanner	hake

C

1 Name a vegetable beginning with **p**.
2 Name a fruit beginning with **g**.
3 Name a fish beginning with **s**.
4 Name a tool beginning with **d**.

Food and drink

Copy these sentences. Use the words in the list below to fill the spaces.

breakfast margarine
butter   marmalade
cereals   milk
cream   muesli
eggs   pudding
flour   sugar
juice   toast
kipper   wheat

A

1 Bread, buns and cakes are made from ____ .

2 Flour is a fine meal or powder made from ____ .

3 Many children have cornflakes, puffed wheat and similar foods for ____ .

4 Such foods are known as ____ .

5 The ____ we eat are laid by hens.

6 Butter, eggs and sugar are used with rice to make a rice ____ .

7 Fruit is boiled with ____ to make jam.

8 Jam made with oranges is called ____ .

B

1 The ____ which we drink comes from the cow.

2 If milk is allowed to stand the ____ rises to the top.

3 The ____ which we spread on our bread is made from milk.

4 Many people eat ____ instead of butter.

5 You make ____ by browning both sides of a slice of bread.

6 The liquid part of fruits and vegetables is called ____ .

7 You can make your own ____ by mixing oats, nuts and dried fruit.

8 A ____ is a salted and smoked herring.

Alphabetical order

All these words begin with a different letter.

fruit
year
march
board
shade

To put them in **a-b-c** or alphabetical order we look at the first letter only.

board
fruit
march
shade
year

All these words begin with the same letter.

bead
black
brick
book
bath

To put them in alphabetical order we must look at the **second** letter in each.

e   l   r   o   a

Now it is easy to put them in their right order.

b**a**th
b**e**ad
b**l**ack
b**o**ok
b**r**ick

A   Write the words in each column in alphabetical order.

1   bank   2   crop   3   loaf
    bend   club   lick
    boat   case   lump
    bite   chop   lamb
    burn   cost   leaf

4   peck   5   slot   6   much
    part   scar   milk
    port   ship   meat
    pure   stop   mask
    pine   safe   more

B   Can you spot the word which is **out of order** in each of these columns?

1   nail   2   gate   3   feel
    nurse   give   from
    near   gone   fine
    nice   glad   flat
    noon   grow   fuss

4   east   5   pray
    edge   pill
    else   plan
    echo   post
    even   punt

C   Put these names in alphabetical order.

John
Janine
James
Joanna
Jeremy
Joseph

The lion and the mouse

A lion was asleep in his den one day when a playful little mouse ran up his outstretched paw and across his nose awakening him from his nap. As quick as lightning the lion clapped his mighty paw upon the frightened little mouse and roared angrily.

"Please don't kill me," squealed the mouse. "Forgive me this time and I will never forget it. One day I may be able to do you a good turn to repay your kindness."

The lion smiled at the mouse, amused by the thought that such a tiny creature could ever be able to help him. So he lifted his paw and let the mouse go.

Later, while the lion was out hunting, he became caught in a net which some men had set to catch him. At once he let out a roar that echoed through the forest. The little mouse heard it, and recognising the voice of the lion who had spared his life, ran to where the king of beasts lay tangled in the net of ropes.

"Well, your majesty," said the mouse, "I know you did not believe me when I said that a day may come when I may repay your kindness, but here is my chance."

At once the little mouse started to nibble through the ropes that bound the lion with his sharp little teeth. Soon the lion was free and able to crawl out of the hunters' snare.

This fable teaches us that no act of kindness, however small, is ever wasted.

1 Which word in the first paragraph means **a short sleep**?
2 How did the mouse wake the lion up?
3 How did the mouse persuade the lion not to kill him?
4 Why was the lion so amused at what the mouse said?
5 What did the men use to catch the lion?
6 How did the mouse recognise the trapped lion?
7 How did the mouse set the lion free?
8 What is the lesson of this fable?
9 Why does thè mouse address the lion as "your majesty"?

Verbs past time

Present time:
We **begin** our holidays today.

Past time:
They **began** their holidays yesterday.

Learn the verbs in this list, then answer the questions.

Present	Past
blow	blew
break	broke
do	did
drive	drove
eat	ate
feel	felt
fly	flew
hide	hid
know	knew
sleep	slept
take	took
tear	tore

A Copy this column. Fill the blanks.

	Present	Past
1	tear	____
2	break	____
3	sleep	____
4	know	____
5	____	took
6	____	hid
7	____	drove
8	____	ate
9	fly	____
10	____	blew
11	do	____
12	____	felt

B Write the verbs in past time which must be used to fill the gaps.

1 Peter ____ a long time to do his sums.

2 Mr. Bond ____ the car into the garage.

3 I went to bed early and ____ all night.

4 The high wind ____ the leaves off the trees.

5 Maria ____ a plate when she washed the dishes.

6 The dog ____ all his food and wanted more.

7 The lark ____ up into the sky.

8 James ____ a pain in his side.

9 Martin ____ the answer to every question.

10 Anne ____ her anorak on a rusty nail.

Birthdays

A   Read this poem, then answer the questions.

Monday's child is fair of face,
Tuesday's child is full of grace,
Wednesday's child is full of woe,
Thursday's child has far to go,
Friday's child is loving and giving,
Saturday's child works hard for its living,
But the child that is born on a Sunday
Is fair and wise and good and gay.

1   Which child has to work hard for a living?

2   The child born on a Tuesday is full of ____ .

3   Which child will be a sad child?

4   Which child will be a pretty child?

5   Which child is loving and giving?

6   Which child will travel a lot?

7   What is the child born on a Sunday like?

B   Write the names of the days of the week in order.

Opposite each day write a sentence about something you do on that day.

Examples

Monday   I take money to school to pay for my dinners for the week.

Tuesday   I borrow a book from the class library.

Saturday   I go shopping with my mother.

Same sound — different meaning

Some words have the same sound as other words, but they differ in spelling and meaning.

Look at these four pairs of words.
Learn to spell each word.
Learn the meaning of each.

hear   You **hear** with your ears.

here   I will wait **here** for you. (*in this place*)

main   The **main** road is the most important one.

mane   The long hair on the neck of a horse or a lion is called a **mane**.

meat   The flesh of an animal used for food is called **meat**.

meet   When people **meet** they get together.

pail   A **pail** is a kind of bucket.

pale   A **pale** person has little colour.

Choose the correct word from the pair above to complete each sentence.

1 **pail   pale**
   She looked very ＿＿＿ after her illness.

2 **meat   meet**
   The ＿＿＿ was too tough to eat.

3 **here   hear**
   We did not ＿＿＿ the postman knocking.

4 **main   mane**
   The school is on the ＿＿＿ road.

5 **pail   pale**
   The ＿＿＿ was half full of water.

6 **main   mane**
   The horse had a very long ＿＿＿ .

7 **meat   meet**
   We will ＿＿＿ you outside the cinema.

The months of the year

	January							February					
S		6	13	20	27				3	10	17	24	
M		7	14	21	28				4	11	18	25	
T	1	8	15	22	29				5	12	19	26	
W	2	9	16	23	30				6	13	20	27	
Th	3	10	17	24	31				7	14	21	28	
F	4	11	18	25				1	8	15	22	29	
S	5	12	19	26				2	9	16	23		

	March							April				
S		2	9	16	23	30			6	13	20	27
M		3	10	17	24	31			7	14	21	28
T		4	11	18	25			1	8	15	22	29
W		5	12	19	26			2	9	16	23	30
Th		6	13	20	27			3	10	17	24	
F		7	14	21	28			4	11	18	25	
S	1	8	15	22	29			5	12	19	26	

	May						June				
S		4	11	18	25		1	8	15	22	29
M		5	12	19	26		2	9	16	23	30
T		6	13	20	27		3	10	17	24	
W		7	14	21	28		4	11	18	25	
Th	1	8	15	22	29		5	12	19	26	
F	2	9	16	23	30		6	13	20	27	
S	3	10	17	24	31		7	14	21	28	

	July							August					
S		6	13	20	27				3	10	17	24	31
M		7	14	21	28				4	11	18	25	
T	1	8	15	22	29				5	12	19	26	
W	2	9	16	23	30				6	13	20	27	
Th	3	10	17	24	31				7	14	21	28	
F	4	11	18	25				1	8	15	22	29	
S	5	12	19	26				2	9	16	23	30	

	September						October				
S		7	14	21	28			5	12	19	26
M	1	8	15	22	29			6	13	20	27
T	2	9	16	23	30			7	14	21	28
W	3	10	17	24			1	8	15	22	29
Th	4	11	18	25			2	9	16	23	30
F	5	12	19	26			3	10	17	24	31
S	6	13	20	27			4	11	18	25	

	November						December				
S		2	9	16	23	30		7	14	21	28
M		3	10	17	24		1	8	15	22	29
T		4	11	18	25		2	9	16	23	30
W		5	12	19	26		3	10	17	24	31
Th		6	13	20	27		4	11	18	25	
F		7	14	21	28		5	12	19	26	
S	1	8	15	22	29		6	13	20	27	

A Look at the calendar. Answer the questions. A year in which February has 29 days is known as a Leap Year.

1 How many months are there in the year?

2 Which month has the shortest name?

3 Write the names of the three months ending with **-ember**.

4 Which month has the longest name?

5 Which month has fewest days?

6 In which month does your birthday come?

7 Name the month in which Christmas comes.

8 Write the names of the four months which have no letter **r** in them.

B We can write the names of most of the months in a short way.

Copy these short forms and learn them.

1 January — Jan.

2 February — Feb.

3 March — Mar.

4 April — April

5 May — May

6 June — June

7 July — July

8 August — Aug.

9 September — Sept.

10 October — Oct.

11 November — Nov.

12 December — Dec.

Writing dates

Write **st** after the number.

1st	first
21st	twenty-first
31st	thirty-first

Write **nd** after the number.

2nd	second
22nd	twenty-second

Write **rd** after the number.

3rd	third
23rd	twenty-third

For all other numbers in the calendar add **th**.

4th	fourth
11th	eleventh
17th	seventeenth
25th	twenty-fifth

A   Use numbers to write these.

1	fifth	6	third	11	thirty-first
2	tenth	7	ninth	12	seventh
3	second	8	twenty-first	13	twenty-third
4	first	9	sixteenth	14	twelfth
5	sixth	10	fourth	15	twenty-second

B   **Writing dates**: 14th May or May 14th

1   Write the date for the twenty-fourth of September.

2   On which date does New Year's Day come?

3   What is the date today?

4   Write the date of your birthday.

5   Write the date for August the twenty-first.

6   On which date does Christmas Day come?

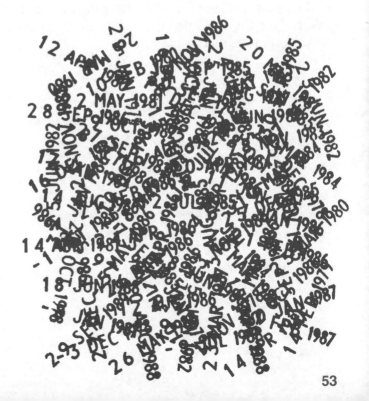

A camping holiday

Last summer Roger and his sister Jill went on a camping holiday in Wales with their parents for the first time. Their new blue tent, which had two bedrooms and a living-room, was pitched in a large field near a sandy bay. There were no other tents in the field and Roger pretended that they were explorers.

Early every morning the two children and their mother went swimming while their father made the breakfast. When they came back, hungry from their exercise, they found him cooking beans and eggs on a portable gas stove. After breakfast they all went down to the beach and played cricket and enjoyed the sunshine.

In the afternoons the children went fishing with their nets in the clear pools, while their parents sat on the sand reading. In the evening they walked to the farmhouse at the foot of the hill. They watched the cows being milked and then had supper with the farmer and his wife. The farmer told the children all about his animals and his crops and promised to let them help with the harvest if they came back in the autumn. At sunset they strolled back along the deserted road to their tent, climbed into their sleeping bags and fell fast asleep. Nothing disturbed them until the singing of the birds woke them next morning.

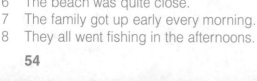

True or false?
Write in your book the statements that are true.
1 Roger and Jill had not been camping before.
2 Their father cooked the supper every evening.
3 The camp site was very crowded.
4 The children slept soundly at night.
5 **Portable** means 'easily carried'.
6 The beach was quite close.
7 The family got up early every morning.
8 They all went fishing in the afternoons.

Rhymes

car   star   bar   tar
far   jar   are   bar
lie   nigh   shy   high
sly   pie   sky   sty

let   set   bet   net
pet   met   wet   yet
tight   fight   sight   light
right   night   might   white

A   Read this poem carefully. Then copy it, putting in the words which you think will end each line.

Twinkle, twinkle, little ____ .
How I wonder what you ____ !
Up above the world so ____
Like a diamond in the ____ .

When the blazing sun is ____ ,
And the grass with dew is ____ ,
Then you show your little ____ .
Twinkle, twinkle, all the ____ .

B   Write the list of words in capital letters. After each word write the three words in small letters which will rhyme with it.

Example   1   LATE   gate, weight, wait

1   LATE   mend   park   stout

2   BARK   gate   pout   sing

3   OUT   cling   weight   lend

4   BEND   mark   about   bring

5   RING   wait   lark   send

C   The missing word in each line below rhymes with the word in bold type.

1   Two pence is a ____ sum of money.   **crawl**

2   I will ____ you at the corner of the street.   **heat**

3   The bread was too ____ to eat.   **nail**

4   If you ____ a dog he may bite you.   **keys**

5   Mum asked Sally to ____ the tea.   **snore**

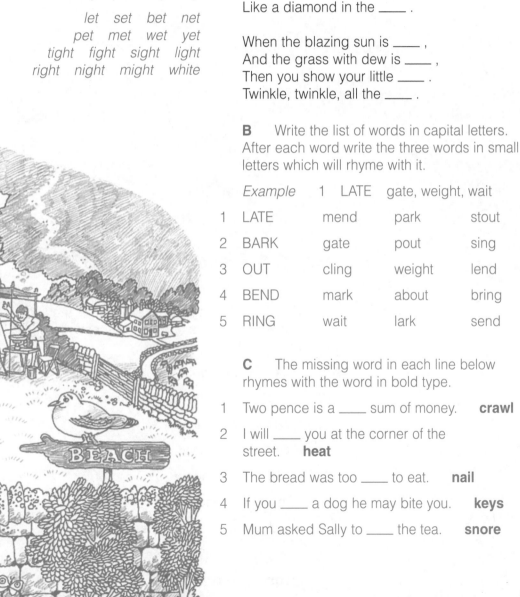

Compound words

A **compound** word is formed by joining together two or more words.

Example
tea+**pot**=**teapot**

A   How many things can you see in the picture whose names are compound words? The list on the left under the picture may help you. Write the name of each object. Show the two words which make up each compound word.

Example   **rail**+**way**=**railway**

armchair
wheelbarrow
birdcage
matchbox
butterfly
silkworm
cowboy
bulldog
hedgehog
snowdrop
dustbin
greenhouse
broomstick
blackboard

B   In each line below, join together the two words in bold type to form a compound word. Start with the second word.

1   a **fish** which is **gold** in colour

2   a **boat** which is driven by a **motor**

3   a **shade** over a **lamp**

4   a **cloth** which covers a **table**

5   a **ball** made of **snow**

6   a **room** for a **bed**

7   **weed** which grows in the **sea**

8   a **tray** to hold cigarette **ash**

9   a **box** for keeping **cash**

The long and the short

There is a short way of writing some words.

Avenue	Ave.
Doctor	Dr.
Mistress	Mrs.
Mister	Mr.
Road	Rd.
Square	Sq.
Street	St.
Terrace	Terr.

A   Write each of these the short way:

1   Doctor Smith

2   High Street

3   Mister Lee

4   Station Terrace

5   Mistress Bond

6   Bush Avenue

7   Victoria Square

8   Redlands Road

Initials

Instead of writing a person's first names in full we write only the **first letter**, as a **capital**, followed by a full stop.

Examples

Edward Marsh
E. Marsh

Arthur John Bond
A. J. Bond

Joanna Long
J. Long

B   Draw envelopes in your exercise book and write these names and addresses, using initials and the short forms you have learnt.

1   Mister Ronald Green, of 12 Church Street, Camford, CP20 3NF.

2   Mistress Jane Everson, of 9 Norton Road, Benham, BP13 4QT.

3   Miss Eva May Brent, of 16 Park Terrace, Broxley, BI58 2RV.

4   Doctor Ann June Johnson, of 25 Poplar Avenue, Reddington, RN41 9GH.

5   Mister Sanjay Prasad, of 31 Chester Square, Podworth, PE57 9AL.

Short forms

The short way of writing **has not** is **hasn't**.
We can also write **that is** a short way – **that's**.

In a similar way the word **will** can be added to words and written in a short way.

I will	I'll
you will	you'll
he will	he'll
she will	she'll
we will	we'll
they will	they'll

Remember that the **'** shows that the letters **wi** have been left out.

A   Write the short form for:

1	is not	6	do not	11	I will
2	we will	7	where is	12	does not
3	here is	8	you will	13	it is
4	he will	9	did not	14	she will
5	are not	10	they will	15	what is

B   Write the short form of the two words in bold type in these sentences.

1   I know **you will** be pleased with your present.

2   Nishani says **there is** plenty of time.

3   Next time **we will** go by train.

4   We must find out **who is** going to the party.

5   I promise you **I will** do my best.

6   If Melanie is late **she will** be scolded.

7   The boys say **they will** call on their way home.

8   Aled **would not** get up when called.

9   It is very likely **he will** be late for school.

10   Everybody says **it is** a fine drawing.

C   Change these short forms back into two words.

1	haven't	6	couldn't
2	he'll	7	it's
3	don't	8	she'll
4	she's	9	shouldn't
5	didn't	10	wasn't

Similars

A **plucky** sailor

A **brave** sailor

The words **plucky** and **brave** are similar in meaning.

Learn the list of similars, then answer the questions.

aged	old
connect	join
glance	look
loiter	linger
slender	slim
cash	money
garments	clothes
handsome	beautiful
plump	fat
tremble	shake

A For each word in bold type give a word which has a similar meaning.

1 The **cash** was taken to the bank.

2 The plumber came to **connect** the pipes.

3 He is a very **handsome** child.

4 The Browns had a **plump** turkey for Christmas.

5 You should not **loiter** on the way home.

6 He did not even **glance** at the book.

7 The dancer has a **slender** figure.

8 The door was opened by an **aged** man.

9 The trains made the old bridge **tremble**.

10 All **garments** sold in this shop are tailor made.

B Write simpler words which are similar in meaning to these. Some you learnt in Book 1.

1	broad	9	commence
2	plucky	10	reply
3	finish	11	wealthy
4	large	12	weeping
5	repair	13	correct
6	collect	14	peril
7	difficult	15	assist
8	stout	16	farewell

Androcles and the lion

Once, long ago, a shepherd was roaming the hot, desert land of Africa when he met a lion. He was very frightened, but when he saw that the lion had a thorn in its paw and was in terrible pain he walked towards it, spoke to it gently and pulled out the thorn. From that time on, Androcles and the lion were great friends.

Some time later some soldiers came and arrested Androcles. They took him far across the sea to the great city of Rome. The Emperor of Rome tried to make Androcles give up his Christian faith, and when he refused had him thrown into a huge arena to be torn apart and eaten by a fierce lion.

Androcles saw the lion spring towards him. Then, suddenly, the lion stopped, bowed its head and held out its paw. Androcles knew then that this lion was his friend from the desert of Africa who had been captured by hunters and brought to Rome.

The Emperor was amazed. "You and your lion have been loyal and brave, Androcles," he said. "You shall both be released at once."

So Androcles and the lion returned across the sea to their home in the desert land of Africa.

1 In which country did Androcles first meet the lion?
2 What work did Androcles do for his living?
3 How did Androcles feel when he first saw the lion?
4 What does **arrested** mean?
5 How do you know the Emperor of Rome was not a Christian?
6 How did the Emperor plan to punish Androcles?
7 Why did the Emperor release Androcles and the lion?
8 Where did they go when they were released?
9 Androcles was loyal and brave. Write a sentence to say what else you think he was, and why you think this.

Fun with words

In each group of words on the right are two pairs of words and one odd word.

You have to find the word which will make up the third pair.

Look at the first pair of words in **A**: **ten   tent**.

The second word is made by writing the letter **t** after the first word.

Look at the second pair. The second word is again formed by writing **t** after the first word: **sea   seat**.

To find the missing word write **t** after the odd word.

Example   **star   start**

A   Now find the other missing words. In each group a different letter must be added.

1   ten   tent   2   pan   pane   3   bun   bung
    sea   seat   hop   hope   ran   rang
    star   hid   thin

4   ten   tend   5   tea   team
    ban   band   for   form
    win   war

B   From the letters in the word **tens** we can make the word **nest**.

From the letters in the words in bold type make words which will fit into the spaces below.

1   There were five eggs in the ____ .   **tens**

2   The smallest pony was quite ____ .   **meat**

3   The journey was a very ____ one.   **owls**

4   Every child should learn to ____ well.   **dare**

5   We should take great ____ with our spelling.   **race**

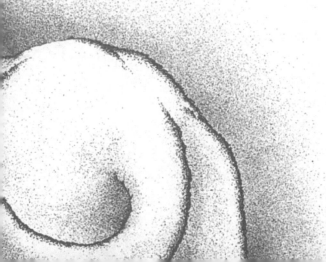

More fun with words

A   Each dash in these sentences stands for a letter.
Each group of letters spells a word.

Example
Mary has long g _ _ _ en hair.
The missing letters are **old**.

Each missing word has **three** letters. Write the missing words only.

1   The plants were bl _ _ _ down by the strong wind.

2   Pigs g _ _ _ t when they eat their food.

3   The little boy sat down on the three-legged s _ _ _ l.

4   We sometimes have snow in the _ _ _ ter.

5   Wolves were h _ _ _ ing in the forest.

6   The _ _ _ tain of the ship was a Dane.

7   The mon _ _ _ hung from the tree by his long tail.

B   Each missing word has **four** letters. Write the missing words only.

1   Wendy's class will have a new t _ _ _ _ er next term.

2   Bees had s _ _ _ _ ed on an apple tree in the garden.

3   The tired horse was taken to the st _ _ _ _ _ .

4   Mum turned on the heater because the room was c _ _ _ _ y.

5   The engine was letting off s _ _ _ _ _ .

6   We saw the p _ _ _ _ landing on the runway.

7   The express t _ _ _ _ ran off the rails.

Verbs past time

Present time:
I **feel** a pain in my side today.

Past time:
I **felt** a pain in my side yesterday.

Learn the words in this list, then answer the questions.

Present	Past
build	built
creep	crept
grow	grew
ride	rode
ring	rang
rise	rose
see	saw
sink	sank
speak	spoke
steal	stole

A   Copy these columns. Fill the blanks.

	Present	Past
1	___	saw
2	___	rang
3	___	rose
4	___	grew
5	___	sank
6	speak	___
7	steal	___
8	ride	___
9	build	___
10	creep	___

B   Write the verbs in past time which will fill the gaps.

1   He ___ to the seaside on his new bicycle.

2   The boat filled with water and ___ .

3   The boy ___ the school bell.

4   The gardener ___ some beautiful roses.

5   I ___ to him on the telephone.

6   The boys ___ a sandcastle on the beach.

7   We ___ two bear cubs in the zoo.

8   The thief ___ the money from the till.

9   The sun ___ at six o'clock yesterday morning.

10   The burglar ___ quietly into the house.

Using took and taken

I **took** a book home.

I **have taken** a book home.

(**have** helps the word **taken**)

The book **was taken** home

(**was** helps the word **taken**)

The word **took** needs no helping word.

The word **taken** always has a helping word:

is taken
was taken
are taken
were taken
has taken
have taken
had taken
will be taken

A   Use **took** or **taken** to fill each space.

1   It was ____
2   You ____
3   He has ____
4   I ____
5   They are ____
6   You have ____
7   He ____
8   We were ____
9   It will be ____
10 She ____

B   Fill each space with **took** or **taken**.

1   The man was ____ ill at the football match.
2   They ____ the man to the hospital.
3   Bela ____ her cocoa to bed with her.
4   She ____ two pills after dinner.
5   The thief ____ all the money in the house.
6   Carly has ____ great care with her work.
7   The two men were ____ to prison.
8   After Alan had ____ his shoes to the shoe repairer he went fishing.
9   As it was raining Ramu ____ his umbrella.
10 The dustmen have ____ the rubbish away.

When people speak

Look at this sentence:

"This orange is sour," said Robert.

The words spoken by Robert were
This orange is sour.

Notice the speech marks come before the first word spoken **"This** … and after the last word spoken … **sour,"**

Notice that the speech marks come after the comma:
… **sour,"**

The speech marks would also come after a question mark:

"Is the orange sour?" asked Robert.

A   Copy these sentences. Put in the speech marks.

1   Pass me the sugar, please, said Mrs. Norland.

2   Are you tired? asked the teacher.

3   I can see you, shouted Ben.

4   Please, Mummy, may I have an apple? begged Simon.

5   Come here, Spot, said the little boy to his dog.

6   I don't want to go to bed yet, said Sandra with a pout.

7   Hurry up, Lila, or you'll be late, said her mother.

8   Spare a penny for the guy, please? asked the two boys.

9   Here is fifty pence for you, replied the man.

10   Be quiet, baby's sleeping, whispered Jemma's mother.

B   Write three sentences of your own in which there are words spoken by people.

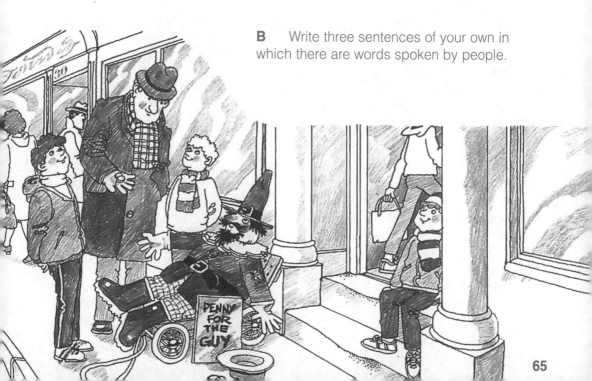

John and the cherries

One day John went shopping with his mother. Their first call was at the greengrocer's, and while his mother was buying some fruit John looked longingly at a box containing lovely red cherries.

"Help yourself to a handful, John," said the greengrocer, but John did not move.

"I'm sure you like cherries, don't you?" asked the puzzled shopkeeper, and John nodded his head quickly. Thinking that the boy was too shy to help himself the greengrocer went to the box and gave John a large handful.

When they had left the shop John's mother asked him why he had not taken the cherries when the greengrocer had told him to.

"Well, you see, Mummy," replied John, "his hand is twice as big as mine."

1 At what shop did John and his mother call first?
2 Explain what looking **longingly** means.
3 What did the greengrocer tell John to do?
4 Did John do as he was told?
5 What did the greengrocer do when he saw John was so shy?
6 Which word describes John best? Why?
clever   greedy   rude   cunning

66

Write the missing words

A

1   A sheep is covered with ____ .
    A rabbit is covered with ____ .

2   A young cat is called a ____ .
    A young dog is called a ____ .

3   A dog barks.
    A lion ____ .

4   The meat from a cow is called ____ .
    The meat from a sheep is called ____ .

5   A bus travels on land.
    A ship travels on ____ .

6   Mr. is a short way of writing Mister.
    Dr. is a short way of writing ____ .

7   You see with your eyes.
    You smell with your ____ .

8   Your foot is at the end of your ____ .
    Your hand is at the end of your ____ .

B   We can put these pairs of statements in a different way.

For the first pair we can write:

Sheep is to **wool** as **rabbit** is to ____ .

The answer is **fur**, as you already know.

Now write the missing words.

1   **Cat** is to **kitten** as **dog** is to ____ .

2   **Dog** is to **bark** as **lion** is to ____ .

3   **Cow** is to **beef** as **sheep** is to ____ .

4   **Ship** is to **sea** as **bus** is to ____ .

5   **Mr.** is to **Mister** as **Dr.** is to ____ .

6   **See** is to **eyes** as **smell** is to ____ .

Compound words

A **compound word** is made up of two or more words.
tooth+**brush**=**toothbrush**

Examples
cowboy
lighthouse
snowdrop
matchbox

A Write the names of six objects in the picture whose names are compound words. Show the two words from which each has been built up.

FOOTPATH

B In each line join the two words in bold type, beginning with the second of them.

1 the **light** given by the **sun**

2 **paper** which is stuck on a **wall** of a room

3 the **teacher** who is **head** of a school

4 part of a bike to **guard** cyclists from **mud**

5 the **pole** to which a **flag** is attached

6 the **stick** to which a **broom** is fastened

7 the **yard** outside a **farm**

8 a **dress** worn by girls and women at **night**

9 a **room** for a **class** of children

Joining sentences using conjunctions

Paul closed his book.
He put it away. *two sentences*

Paul closed his book **and** put
it away. *one sentence*

The word **and** joins the two
sentences.

**A word which joins two
groups of words or two
sentences is called a
conjunction.**

and
but
or
for
as
since
because
while
when
before
after
until
if
whether
unless
where
although

A   Join each pair of sentences below, using a
suitable conjunction from the list on the left.

1   The boy got out of bed.
He stretched his arms.

2   We intended to swim.
The water was too cold.

3   We went to bed early.
We were so tired.

4   The children made their way home.
It was getting dark.

5   Ben made some tea.
His mother bathed the baby.

6   Do your homework.
Have your tea.

7   She was very unpopular.
She was so sarcastic.

8   You can do it yourself.
You are so clever.

B   Insert a suitable conjunction in each
space.

1   Would you like a cup of tea ____ would you
prefer coffee?

2   There will be more accidents at the crossroads
____ a roundabout is built there soon.

3   ____ it poured with rain all day, everyone
enjoyed the outing.

4   I enjoyed the film ____ I had seen it before.

5   We intend to go ____ it snows or not.

6   Please do nothing ____ you hear from me.

7   The pupils visited St. Paul's Cathedral ____ they
were shown the Whispering Gallery.

Using the right verb

bandage
catch
drive
fight
learn
plant
play
roast
row
strike

A Write the verb in the list on the left which fits each space.

1 to ____ a boat   6 to ____ a cold

2 to ____ meat   7 to ____ a game

3 to ____ a car   8 to ____ a battle

4 to ____ a tree   9 to ____ a cut

5 to ____ a lesson   10 to ____ a blow

built
mounted
wrapped
returned
sheltered
spent
stamped
taught
thanked
warmed

B Choose the right word from the list on the left to finish each sentence.

1 We ____ from the rain in an old barn.

2 James ____ from his holiday yesterday.

3 The carol singers ____ their feet to get warm.

4 Dad ____ me to ride a bicycle.

5 Mel has ____ all her money.

6 I ____ the present and gave it to Michael.

7 Maria ____ herself by the blazing fire.

8 The new house was ____ in less than six months.

9 I ____ my aunt for the money she sent me.

10 The cowboy ____ his horse and rode off.

C Use each pair of words in a sentence of your own.

1 bought sweets   4 burnt toast

2 sang carol   5 drank tea

3 posted letter   6 rang bell

Where they live

den
sty
web
nest
cage
hive
hutch
shell
kennel
stable

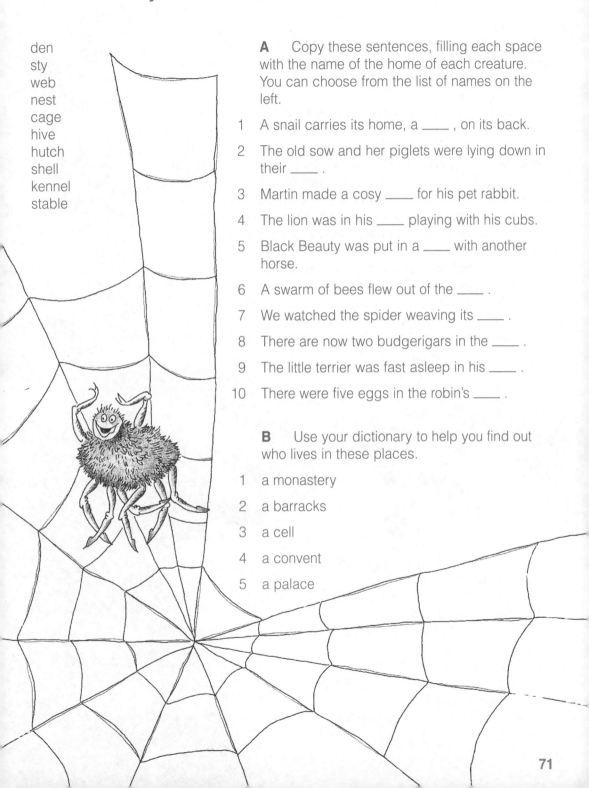

A   Copy these sentences, filling each space with the name of the home of each creature. You can choose from the list of names on the left.

1   A snail carries its home, a ____ , on its back.

2   The old sow and her piglets were lying down in their ____ .

3   Martin made a cosy ____ for his pet rabbit.

4   The lion was in his ____ playing with his cubs.

5   Black Beauty was put in a ____ with another horse.

6   A swarm of bees flew out of the ____ .

7   We watched the spider weaving its ____ .

8   There are now two budgerigars in the ____ .

9   The little terrier was fast asleep in his ____ .

10   There were five eggs in the robin's ____ .

B   Use your dictionary to help you find out who lives in these places.

1   a monastery

2   a barracks

3   a cell

4   a convent

5   a palace

Black Beauty and Ginger

My master and mistress made up their minds to pay a visit to some friends who lived about forty-six miles from our home. James was to drive them in the carriage, which was to be drawn by Ginger and me.

The first day we travelled thirty-two miles. There were some long, steep hills, but James drove so carefully that we were never tired or troubled. He never forgot to put on the brake as we went downhill, nor to take it off at the right place. He kept our feet on the smoothest part of the road; and if the uphill was very long he set the wheels a little across the road, so that the carriage should not run back, and gave us time to breathe. All these little things, together with kind words, help a horse very much.

We stopped once or twice on the road; and just as the sun was going down, we reached the town where we were to spend the night. We stopped at the biggest hotel, which was in the Market Place. We drove under an archway into a long yard, at the end of which were the stables where we were to rest.

Black Beauty   Anna Sewell

1   What did Black Beauty's master and mistress make up their minds to do?
2   How far did they travel the first day?
3   Why were the horses never tired or troubled?
4   What did James do as they went downhill?
5   Why did James set the carriage wheels across the road when going up a long hill?
6   At what time of day did they reach the town?
7   Where did they stop?
8   Where were the stables in which the two horses were to spend the night?

Using ate and eaten

George **ate** his apple.

George **has eaten** his apple.

(**has** helps the word **eaten**)

The apple **was eaten** by George.

(**was** helps the word **eaten**)

The word **ate** needs no helping word.

The word **eaten** always has a helping word:

has eaten
have eaten
is eaten
are eaten
was eaten
were eaten
had eaten
and so on.

A   Use **ate** or **eaten** to fill each space.

1   I ____
2   You have ____
3   It was ____
4   He ____
5   You ____

6   He has ____
7   We ____
8   They are ____
9   She ____
10 We had ____

B   Fill each space with **ate** or **eaten**.

1   John ____ his supper and went to bed.
2   After John had ____ his supper he went to bed.
3   Many meals are ____ on the beach in summer.
4   The monkey ____ all the nuts the children gave him.
5   The sweater was ____ by moths.
6   The little bear's porridge had been ____ by Goldilocks.
7   The puppy ____ his food and looked for more.
8   When you have ____ your food you may leave the table.
9   Esam ____ the icing and left the cake.
10 Bread is ____ all over the world.

C   Complete these sentences.

1   Eat . . . .
2   . . . . has eaten . . . .?
3   . . . . ate . . . .

Rhymes

mouse
house
eyes
rise
day
way
hall
wall
quays
trees
noon
moon

The last word has been left out of each line in this poem. You will find these rhyming words in the list on the left.

A   Copy the poem, filling in the missing words.

The moon

The moon has a face like the clock in the ____ ;
She shines on thieves on the garden ____ ,
On streets and fields and harbour ____ ,
And birds asleep in the forks of ____ .

The squalling cat and the squeaking ____ ,
The howling dog by the door of the ____ ,
The bat that lies in bed at ____ ,
All love to be out by the light of the ____ .

But all of the things that belong to the ____
Cuddle to sleep to be out of her ____ ;
And flowers and children close their ____
Till up in the morning the sun shall ____ .

B   In each group below write three other words which rhyme with the word in bold type. The first letters are given to help you.

1 **bat**	2 **lard**	3 **tack**
r _ _	c _ _ _	r _ _ _
h _ _	y _ _ _	bl _ _ _
p _ _	h _ _ _	st _ _ _

4 **and**	5 **bag**	6 **lick**
h _ _ _	fl _ _	p _ _ _
br _ _ _	dr _ _	tr _ _ _
gr _ _ _	st _ _	qu _ _ _

Sentences

A Write the beginning of each sentence. Then choose the ending which will match it.

Example
1 The greedy boy was ill because he had eaten too much.

Beginning	**Ending**
1 The greedy boy was ill	Simon looked hot and tired.
2 It was raining so heavily	the ship of the desert.
3 As Robert was covered with spots	in a dozen.
4 After mowing the lawn	please let me know.
5 The camel is often called	and went off to school.
6 The load carried by a ship	that the ponds were frozen.
7 Paul picked up his satchel	because he had eaten too much.
8 If you want any help	his mother sent for the doctor.
9 The weather was so cold	is called a cargo.
10 There are twelve things	that Brian put on his mackintosh.

B Copy these beginnings. Add your own endings.

1 Roger burst into tears

2 Just as I left the house

3 Every summer

4 Although he is intelligent

C Begin each sentence in your own way.

1 . . . . a very long way from home.

2 . . . . and we were soaking wet.

3 . . . . because he felt so tired.

4 . . . . and everyone laughed.

75

Forming adjectives

Many adjectives are formed by adding **ful** to a noun.

Examples

hope+full=hope**ful**
(full of hope)

joy+full=joy**ful**
(full of joy)

Note that in adding **-full** one **l** is dropped.

beautiful	peaceful
careful	playful
harmful	thankful
helpful	truthful
painful	useful

A Choose from the list on the left the adjective ending with **-ful** which will fill each gap.

1 a kitten which is full of play   a ___ kitten
2 a village in which there is peace   a ___ village
3 a girl of great beauty   a ___ girl
4 a driver who takes great care   a ___ driver
5 a cut which gives much pain   a ___ cut
6 a book which is of great use   a ___ book
7 a friend who gives help   a ___ friend
8 a person who is full of thanks   a ___ person
9 a boy who speaks the truth   a ___ boy
10 a habit which causes harm   a ___ habit

B Add **-ful** to each of these words. Then choose three of the words you have made and use them in sentences of your own; one word in each sentence.

1	shame	4	cheer	7	disgrace
2	delight	5	hope	8	boast
3	wonder	6	hate	9	rest

Opposites change of word

Learn the list of **opposites**, then answer the questions.

always	never
asleep	awake
better	worse
blunt	sharp
cruel	kind
evil	good
heavy	light
less	more
narrow	wide
pull	push

A   Use the **opposite** of the word in bold type to fill each space.

Example   a short story   **long**

1 a ___ knife   **sharp**

2 a ___ master   **kind**

3 he was ___   **asleep**

4 ___ danger   **more**

5 a ___ road   **narrow**

6 a ___ parcel   **light**

7 to ___ the door   **push**

8 ___ tired   **always**

9 a ___ player   **better**

B   You need opposites again here to fill the spaces.

1 That exercise was **easy** but this one is ___ .

2 I am always **polite** but you are very ___ .

3 This is the **cold** tap and that is the ___ one.

4 Your face is **clean** but your hands are ___ .

5 My uncle is very **generous** but my aunt is ___ .

6 As the postman **departed** the window-cleaner ___ .

7 Twenty pupils were **present** and only one pupil was ___ .

8 This road is **dangerous** but that one is ___ .

9 You are **rich** and I am ___ .

10 The answer is either **right** or ___ .

Feeding the Cats

"I'll give "this gravy to the cats,"
    I heard my mother say
in the dark outside the kitchen door;
    but the gravy went astray;
the scrubbing brush she spilt it on
    got up and walked away.

"I hope it's got some friends," Mum said,
    "or perhaps some babies, who
can get their tongues between the prickles –
    a tricky thing to do.
In future when I feed the cats
    I'll feed the hedgehogs too."

Fleur Adcock

Complete these sentences.

1   The mother went into the garden to give the gravy to the ____ .

2   The "scrubbing brush" that walked away was really a ____ .

3   **Tricky** in verse two means ____ .

4   Three words that rhyme in the first verse are ____ , ____ and ____ .

5   Three words that rhyme in the second verse are ____ , ____ and ____ .

6   The title of the poem is ____ .

7   It was written by ____ .

Same sound — different meaning

Some words have the same sound as other words, but they differ in spelling and meaning.

Look at these four pairs of words.
Learn to spell each word.
Learn the meaning of each.

pain   He felt no **pain** when he had his tooth out.

pane   A new **pane** of glass was fixed in the window.

road   Many cars were parked at the side of the **road**.

rode   Ian **rode** to school on his new bicycle.

sail   One **sail** of the ship was torn by the strong wind.

sale   All goods were very cheap at the **sale**.

there   I left the dish **there**. (*in that place*)

their   The two boys had lost **their** pencils. (*belonging to them*)

Choose the correct word from the pair above to complete each sentence.

1 **road   rode**
   The ____ was muddy after the heavy rain.

2 **sail   sale**
   Helen bought the carpet at a ____ .

3 **pain   pane**
   Susan had a ____ in her arm.

4 **road   rode**
   Alan ____ his pony over the fields.

5 **there   their**
   We waited ____ for an hour.

6 **pain   pane**
   The cricket ball broke a ____ in the window.

7 **sail   sale**
   The ____ of the yacht was lowered as it reached the shore.

Containers

A **purse** holds or contains **money**.

A **jug** contains **water**.

Both are called **containers**.

bin
jug
vase
cup
purse
suitcase
basket
teapot
envelope

A Write the names of these containers. Look at the list on the left.

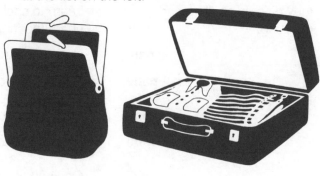

B Copy the sentences. Write the name of a container in each space.

1 Marion had no loose change in her ____ .

2 The ____ was full of rubbish.

3 I drink a ____ of tea at eleven o'clock every morning.

4 There was no milk left in the ____ .

5 Pack your clothes in this ____ .

6 Some people carry their shopping in a ____ .

7 David put the letter in the ____ and posted it.

8 There were some beautiful tulips in the ____ .

C What would these containers contain? Use your dictionary to help you.

1 decanter

2 scabbard

3 portfolio

4 carafe

Using longer words

The word **where** can be joined to **any**, **every**, **no** and **some**.

> any+where=**anywhere**
>
> every+where=**everywhere**
>
> no+where=**nowhere**
>
> some+where=**somewhere**

A   Use one of these longer words to fill each space.

1   The hammer must be ____ in the house.

2   We looked ____ for the lost hammer.

3   The hammer was ____ to be seen.

4   We could not find the hammer ____ .

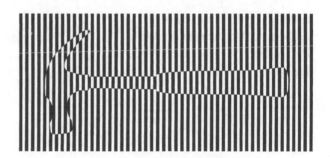

The word **body** can be joined to **any**, **every**, **no** and **some**.

> any+body=**anybody**
>
> every+body=**everybody**
>
> no+body=**nobody**
>
> some+body=**somebody**

B   Write the words which will fill the gaps.

1   I don't think there is ____ at home.

2   We should be kind to ____ .

3   You must get ____ to help you in the garden.

4   Jake knocked at the door but ____ answered.

The word **ever** can be joined to **when**, **where**, **who**, **what**, **how** and **which**.

whenever
wherever
whoever
whatever
however
whichever

C   Write the **-ever** words which will finish these sentences.

1   He never wears a hat ____ cold the weather is.

2   People must buy food ____ it costs.

3   ____ took the money must give it back.

4   You can visit us ____ you like.

5   Jason's dog follows him ____ he goes.

6   Take ____ of the two cakes you want.

Compound words using hyphens

You know that compound words are formed by joining together two or more words (**tea**+**pot**=**teapot**).

Some compound words need hyphens.

Examples
twenty+**eight**=**twenty-eight**
walkie+**talkie**=**walkie-talkie**
happy+**go**+**lucky**=**happy-go-lucky**

A   Join these words together with a hyphen.

1   upside+down

2   stepping+stone

3   forty+six

4   heavy+duty

5   right+handed

B   Join each pair of words below to form a compound word. Decide which ones need hyphens. If you are not sure, check in a dictionary.

1   horse+box

2   clock+work

3   left+handed

4   step+mother

5   hand+kerchief

6   old+fashioned

7   life+boat

8   roller+skate

9   day+dream

10   spot+light

11   skate+board

12   kick+off

13   high+pitched

14   machine+gun

15   make+up

Words with more than one meaning

Some words have more than one meaning.

We went to visit an old tin **mine** in Cornwall.

The red towel is **mine** but the blue one belongs to Sally.

blind
felt
foot
long
mean
ring
rock
suit
top
trunk

A Use the words in the list on the left to fill these spaces. The same word must be used for each pair of sentences.

1 The dress is too ____ so I must shorten it.
I often ____ for a holiday in Spain.

2 The miser was too ____ to buy food for himself.
Some words ____ much the same as other words.

3 I think this dress will ____ you.
Henry wore a navy blue ____ at the wedding.

4 Under the carpet was a layer of ____ .
Kamal ____ ill, so she went to bed early.

5 A ____ person cannot see.
She pulled the ____ down over the window.

6 Mum packed the ____ for the holidays.
The elephant took the bun with his long ____ .

7 There was a hostel at the ____ of the mountain.
He was lame because he had hurt his ____ .

8 Please ____ the doorbell.
Emma wore a ____ on each finger.

9 On the beach was a huge ____ .
Jane tried to ____ the baby to sleep.

10 Humpty Dumpty was sitting on ____ of the wall.
The red ____ was spinning round and round.

B Make up sentences to show that each of these words has two meanings.

1 box

2 letter

3 wood

4 stick

5 match

A bear cub's adventure

Bears have an excellent sense of smell, and very keen hearing;
… and scent the faintest odour from a great distance. This is
fortunate for them, as they are very short-sighted.

A breeze arose, wafting the odour of something sweet
towards Mishook the bear cub. What could it be? The cub did
not know, but his mother and the elder ones recognised the
aroma of honey…

With hurried steps the whole bear family set off in search
of the prize. They trotted along for about a kilometre before
they reached the old decayed tree-trunk where the bees had
taken up their abode. The poor bees saw the plunderers, and
immediately sounded an alarm. They then defended their
store of honey … by fiercely stinging the bears.

But the mother bear and her cubs … calmly continued
their feast of honey, their thick fur protecting them against
the attacks of the bees. One angry bee, however, plunged its
sting into Mishook's nose. He growled furiously, shook his
head, jumped, snorted, turned round like a spinning-top, and
it was with great difficulty that he managed to beat off the
troublesome insect with his paws. But this repulse did not by
any means prevent him from tasting his share of the honey, of
which he immediately became very fond.

Baby Mishook   Leon Golschmann

1   Bears have two senses which are better
    developed than the others. What are they?
2   Why are the bears fortunate in having these
    senses?
3   What was the odour which the breeze blew
    towards Mishook?
4   Where had the bees made their nest?
5   What does **sounded an alarm** mean?
6   How did the bees defend their store of honey?
7   Why were the bears able to continue their feast
    of honey?
8   Which of the bear family was stung by an angry
    bee?
9   The bear tried to get rid of the bee by doing six
    different things. Which one was successful?

The meaning of prefixes mono-, bi-, tri-

A **prefix** is a syllable or syllables joined to the **beginning** of a word.

Understanding the meaning of the prefix helps you understand the meaning of the word.

Use your dictionary to help you understand the meaning of the prefixes in these words.

mono- means ONE

Example
Monoplane – an aeroplane with **one** pair of wings.

A

1 What kind of word is a monosyllable?

2 What kind of voice is monotonous?

3 What kind of railway is a monorail?

4 What kind of monument is a monolith?

bi- means TWO

Example
Bicycle – a cycle with **two** wheels.

B

1 A biped has two _____ .

2 A bivalve has two _____ .

3 To bisect is to cut into two _____ .

4 Binoculars have two _____ .

tri- means THREE

Example
Tripod – a stand with **three** legs.

C

1 A triangle has three _____ .

2 A tricycle has three _____ .

3 Triennial means happening every three _____ .

4 A trireme is a galley (ship) with three _____ .

D   What is the meaning of these words?

1 bilingual   4 monogram

2 triplets   5 trident

3 biplane

Using gave and given

Aunt Judy **gave** Paul fifty pence.

Aunt Judy **has given** Paul fifty pence.

(**has** helps the word **given**)

Paul **was given** fifty pence by Aunt Judy.

(**was** helps the word **given**)

The word **gave** needs no helping word.

The word **given** always has a helping word:

has given
have given
is given
are given
was given
were given
had given
and so on.

A   Use **gave** and **given** to fill each space.

1   He has ___
2   She ___
3   It was ___
4   You ___
5   They had ___
6   We have ___
7   I ___
8   They have ___
9   They were ___
10   We ___

B   Write the word which fills each space.

1   The teacher ___ each child a new pencil.
2   Each child was ___ a new pencil.
3   All the pens were ___ out.
4   Ann has ___ Beth a sweet.
5   Terry ___ me a big red apple.

 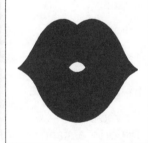

6   Jennifer ___ her parents a kiss before going to bed.
7   Every child at the party will be ___ a toy.
8   Wai was sorry that she had ___ all her sweets away.
9   Harjit liked the bat which Uncle Yusuf ___ him.

Things which are alike

When something is very light in weight we say it is as **light** as a **feather**.

This is because a feather is so very, very light.

Learn the sayings in the list below.

as black as pitch
as brown as a berry
as easy as A B C
as green as grass
as hard as nails
as hot as fire
as soft as putty
as sour as vinegar
as stiff as a poker
as weak as a kitten

A   Write the missing words.

1   as weak as a ___   6   as hard as ___

2   as sour as ___   7   as stiff as a ___

3   as easy as ___   8   as soft as ___

4   as brown as a ___   9   as black as ___

5   as green as ___   10   as hot as ___

B   Now think of some new comparisons and avoid using the sayings on the left.

1   as black as . . . .

2   as easy as . . . .

3   as difficult as . . . .

4   as hot as . . . .

5   as happy as . . . .

C   Complete these sentences with comparisons so descriptive and so convincing that your reader knows exactly how you felt when each incident happened.

1   The vicious cat's claws sank into my arm like . . . .

2   When I told my mother the news, she turned as pale as . . . .

3   When I had to read in assembly, my heart was beating like . . . .

4   I was so frightened that my stomach felt as if . . . .

Opposites using un, in, im

The opposite of certain words can be formed by adding **un**, **in**, or **im**.

Adding un

certain	uncertain
comfortable	uncomfortable
common	uncommon
conscious	unconscious
healthy	unhealthy
pleasant	unpleasant
selfish	unselfish
steady	unsteady
suitable	unsuitable
truthful	untruthful
used	unused
wise	unwise

Adding in or im

capable	incapable
complete	incomplete
convenient	inconvenient
correct	incorrect
curable	incurable
direct	indirect
secure	insecure
sufficient	insufficient
visible	invisible
movable	immovable
possible	impossible
pure	impure

A Write the opposites of these words.

1 secure
2 selfish
3 pure
4 common
5 capable
6 certain
7 direct
8 pleasant
9 convenient
10 correct

11 sufficient
12 healthy
13 movable
14 used
15 visible
16 steady
17 possible
18 suitable
19 wise
20 complete

B Use your dictionary and decide which word in the lists of opposites best describes:

1 a person who frequently tells lies

2 a salary which is not enough to live on

3 something which cannot be seen

4 a person who is frequently ill

5 a person who puts others before himself

6 a pack of cards from which some are missing

7 a rock which cannot be moved

8 a disease which cannot be cured

9 a sum in which there is a mistake

10 a person who has fainted

Using adjectives

1 The man walked down the road.

2 The **old** man walked down the road.

Sentence 2 is better than sentence 1 because it tells us something about the man. He was **old**.

3 The **old** man walked down the **dusty** road.

This is better than either 1 or 2 because it also tells us something about the road. It was **dusty**.

angry
blazing
brave
clever
cold
cosy
damaged
delicious
foggy
frightened
hungry
kind
lovely
naughty
nearby
pretty
ripe
savage
stormy
straying

A Copy these sentences, filling each space with a suitable adjective from the list on the left.

1 The ＿＿ girl wore a ＿＿ dress.

2 The ＿＿ huntsman enjoyed the ＿＿ dinner.

3 A ＿＿ dog was snarling at the ＿＿ boy.

4 It was a ＿＿ night.

5 The ＿＿ sailor dived into the ＿＿ sea to save his mate.

6 The pear was perfectly ＿＿ .

7 There was a ＿＿ fire in the ＿＿ kitchen.

8 The ＿＿ car was towed to a ＿＿ garage.

9 The ＿＿ sheepdog rounded up the ＿＿ sheep.

10 The ＿＿ father punished his ＿＿ son.

B Make sentences of your own from these words, putting two adjectives in each.

1 man; won; prize

2 baby; played; rattle

3 sun; shone; sky

4 ship; wrecked; shore

5 shopkeeper; served; customer

6 cat; chased; mouse

C Complete these sentences.

1 The shy girl . . . .

2 The blazing sun . . . .

3 The noisy car . . . .

4 The slimy creature . . . .

The faithful collie

James Hogg was a well-known poet, but he was also a shepherd. One night, when he was out with his sheep, it started to snow heavily. Knowing that he would have to get his flock in, Hogg whistled for his faithful collie. When she came running to him, he told her to get all the sheep in from one side of the moor while he did the same on the other side. Off they both went.

The shepherd returned much later, bringing with him the sheep he had rounded up. As there was no sign of the collie, he went into his cabin to wait.

After several hours a painful whine and a feeble scratching were heard at the door. Rushing out, the shepherd saw that the collie had brought in her share of the flock with not a single sheep missing. Then he noticed that the collie carried something in her mouth. He called her and she came and laid at his feet a new-born puppy.

Off she went into the snow again, but soon returned with another puppy, but as she took this to her master she fell to the ground and died. James Hogg knew that although his faithful collie had had her puppies in a snowstorm she had carried out her duty to her master and had brought the sheep safely home.

1 What work did James Hogg do besides writing poetry?
2 What happened when he was out with his sheep one night?
3 How did the shepherd call his collie?
4 What did he tell her to do?
5 What did the shepherd do when he returned with the sheep?
6 What did he hear at the door of his cabin after waiting for several hours?
7 What did he see when he rushed out?
8 Continue the story. Write six more sentences saying what James Hogg did next and how he felt.